PUT OUT THE
FIRE

EDDIE SPENCER

WITH LAFON WALCOTT BURROW

PUT OUT THE
FIRE

HOW TO CONTROL YOUR ANGER
BEFORE IT DESTROYS YOUR LIFE

REDEMPTION PRESS

Redemption Press (PO Box 427, Enumclaw, WA 98022) functions only as book publisher. As such, the ultimate design, content, editorial accuracy, and views expressed or implied in this work are those of the author.

Unless otherwise noted, all Scriptures are taken from the Holy Bible, New International Version, Copyright © 1973, 1978, 1984 by the International Bible Society. Used by permission of Zondervan Publishing House. The "NIV" and "New International Version" trademarks are registered in the United States Patent and Trademark Office by International Bible Society.

Scripture references marked KJV are taken from the King James Version of the Bible.

Scripture references marked NASB are taken from the New American Standard Bible, © 1960, 1963, 1968, 1971, 1972, 1973, 1975, 1977 by The Lockman Foundation. Used by permission.

ISBN 13: 978-1-63232-286-9
Library of Congress Catalog Card Number: 2006908384

Dedication

To my darling wife Betty–I thank God that you are in my life. God has used you to help me to grow into being the man He wants me to be. I appreciate your love, support, commitment, patience and prayers.

To my precious daughter Sharon (Daddy's Baby Girl), and my beloved sons Lincoln and Reginald–I am grateful and privileged that you are a part of my life. My prayer for each of you is that you will be all that the Lord Jesus Christ wants you to be.

To my wonderful and lovely mother Mary Elizabeth Spencer–thank you for never giving up on me and for your unconditional love.

To my brothers and sisters; and to my in-laws Rev. James and Rosie Graves for your support and encouragement.

In Memory

George and Lynda Lee Stock—my brother and sister in Christ—for their friendship and encouragement

Rev. Joel Hayes—my spiritual father—who challenged me to make myself available to be used by the Lord Jesus Christ

Veola Washington–who always gave me advice and words of encouragement when I needed them most

Table of Contents

Acknowledgements

A special thank you to my Lord and Savior Jesus Christ for you, LaFon, and your family. I really do appreciate your wisdom, unconditional support and the encouragement that you have given to me and my family. I will always be indebted to you. I love you "Mom." Thanks once again for helping the manuscript become a reality.

I am also grateful to those who read parts or all of the manuscript and offered suggestions to improve it–Beau and Christy Burrow; Martha Stockstill; my Pastors Joel and Linda Hill at Son Flower Church in Anguilla, MS; Rev. Jerry Clark, Pastor of Riverwood Bible Church in Jackson, MS; Jim Young; Helen-Ruth Hendon; my aunt, Shirley Buckley; and Bobbi Vaughn.

To Ernest Herndon, Gary and Dale Felder, Jim and Toni Wild, and Keith Ferguson–I thank you for encouraging me to put this in book form. You all know that I first presented this material as a workshop for an anger management class.

I thank God for my prayer warriors–Robert and Blanche Williams, Rev. Harvest and Annie Johnson, the Alta Woods United Methodist Church family in Jackson, MS, the White Oak United Methodist Church family in Crystal Springs, MS and the Riverwood Bible Church family in Jackson, MS.

I owe much gratitude to Jan Farrington, Mary Elizabeth Smith, Judith Travis and all others associated with the Support Development Organization, Inc.

Last, but not least, I thank God for Leigh Holland and his family. Leigh, I thank you for coming into the prison in 1982 and teaching me how to read and how to trust the Lord with my fears.

Preface

ave you ever said any of the following things to yourself or to somebody else?

- I run my own life. You can't tell me what to do.
- Right this minute I'm so angry I could kill you.
- I will never apologize for what I've done. Never.
- If you don't like who I am, that's too bad; I can't change.
- Who do you think you are, you stupid so-and-so? You can't do that to me!
- Whatever you do to me, I'm gonna do right back to you.
- I may forgive, but I won't forget. Not ever.

If you have, then this is the book for you. Its purpose is to take a look at the problem of anger and how it affects your life and the lives of those around you, and then offer you a proven solution for dealing effectively with your anger. It's designed to be useful to you whether you are a man or a woman, a young person or an adult, a true believer in God or a total skeptic who doesn't yet know Jesus Christ.

This three-part study guide begins by discussing five heart attitudes that set off anger, goes on to consider eight negative effects of uncontrolled anger in your life, and concludes by sharing seven steps you must take in order to deal with your anger before it destroys you, your family, and your future.

Each chapter in the book takes a persuasive look at some things the Bible has to say about anger as well as some of the author's own life experiences and then moves on to make things more personal to you. Through a series of thought-provoking questions, you will be challenged to think matters over for yourself. Next, you will be asked to take a positive action step designed to help you begin to resolve your anger. Finally, you will be given the opportunity to talk things over with God in prayer and to reflect on the truth of what God's Word has to say regarding you and your anger. How you respond to each of these sections will reveal to you where you are right now in regard to living life God's way, and perhaps motivate you to deal truthfully with the things keeping you in bondage to your destructive anger.

There are several ways you can use this study guide. First, you can read it by yourself. You can do this a chapter at a time or you can read it straight through. How you choose to do it is up to you, but if you elect to read the book all at once, you are more likely to miss the opportunities to make it personal. So, if you decide to do it that way, you would be wise to go back through the book a second time and take longer to do the sections that make it personal.

You can also use this study guide with a group. It would be best to have someone qualified to lead your group; but if you don't, it is possible to use the guide without a leader by reading the material on your own and then discussing it together as a group. To make the study more effective, you might want to be accountable to each other by sharing the results of your efforts to take the action steps. Doing the study with a group will provide a chance for you to encourage one another as well as the opportunity for you to pray for each other.

You could do this study together one-on-one with a counselor, a mentor, your spouse, or your parents. To do this, you would want to set aside a regular time to go over the material in the book. In order for the study to be used effectively in this way, everyone involved must remember this should not be a time to argue with each other or lay blame. Instead, it should be an opportunity to focus on what the study guide has to say to you about anger and then to apply that material to your OWN life or to be supportive of the person who is struggling with anger.

However you decide to use this material, you will find the study informative, effective, and personal to your situation. God understands the struggle you are in, as well as what it will take to set you free from bondage to your angry emotions. Moreover, God deeply desires to bring you out of your present circumstances and into right relationship with Himself and the people around you.

Just give God a chance; He can do what you can't do on your own.

About The Author

I f anyone knows what anger can cost you, it's Eddie Charles Spencer. It nearly destroyed his whole life.

The seventh of eleven children, Eddie was born in 1962 in Hollandale, a Mississippi Delta plantation town, where he grew up among the poorest of the poor. He and the rest of his large family lived all jammed up in a shabby three room shack with no indoor plumbing and no air-conditioning. Even as a child, he felt the hopelessness in the world around him where black folks lived trapped in poverty and rejection. Eddie also experienced the abuse of his father who took his own frustrations out on his son.

It didn't take long for Eddie to grow angry himself. Life-changing rage first showed up when he was six years old. His only pair of shoes had fallen apart and his mother sent him off to school wearing his sister's shoes. As he stepped into his first grade classroom, classmates taunted him: "Look at Eddie Spencer. He's got little girl shoes on!" Humiliation and revenge gripped his young mind and launched him on a journey of crime and violence that began at school and quickly spread to the streets. He was arrested the first time when he was seven years old and spent his first night in jail at nine. Before he turned fifteen, he had dropped out of school, been shot four times, been sentenced to training school six times, and even tried to shoot his abusive father. Addicted to drugs and robbing to support that habit, the teenager's anger escalated to violence that spiraled out of control and kept him in trouble with the law. In 1980, just short of his seventeenth birthday, he found himself standing before a judge receiving ten years mandatory at Parchman Penitentiary for armed robbery and attempted murder.

Being locked up at Parchman only fueled Eddie's anger and made him more determined no one would get the best of him. Trying to earn himself a prison reputation, he began to box and became a loan-shark. These activities earned him the name he wanted, but eventually took him to the place he decided to murder two men just to increase his reputation. As he sat on his prison cot fingering his homemade knife contemplating that murder, he remembered the words of one of his robbery victims: "You can have the money, but what you really need is to give your life to the Lord Jesus Christ."

Immediately, Eddie knew what he must do. He put away his "shank" and made the choice that changed his heart and gave him a new start at life.

Paroled from prison in 1988, Eddie Spencer is now an ordained minister of the gospel and motivational speaker. In the years since he left jail, he has attended Belhaven College, served as urban director of Young Life Jackson, owned several restaurants, worked with St. Andrews Mission in McComb, MS, and served as a pastor at Alta Woods United Methodist Church in Jackson and White Oak United Methodist Church in Crystal Springs, MS.

In 1990, Eddie was honored by USA Today as one of its fifty national drug-fighting heroes. He was also selected to be a part of the Presidential Drug Task Force, and awarded the WLBT-TV3 "Catch the Spirit" Award. The story of his life is told in the book *INMATE 46857: If God Can Change Me, He Can Change Anybody*, which he co-authored with LaFon Walcott Burrow, as well as included in the book *The Day I Met God*.

Eddie is married and has a daughter and two sons.

A Word From The Author Before You Begin

I am convinced this study can make a difference in your life, but before you begin, I want to talk with you about two ways of thinking which can keep you from dealing with your anger.

The first mindset that will prevent you from overcoming anger is refusing to recognize you have a problem. The truth is until you and I are willing to admit there's something wrong in our lives, we will never do anything about it.

When I was growing up, people used to say to me, "Eddie, you need to get your anger under control before you hurt somebody or destroy your own life." Only I wouldn't listen. Because I was in denial, I wasn't interested in recognizing or dealing with the problems in my life, and I didn't want to hear what anybody had to say to me about my situation.

Proverbs 28:13 says, "He who conceals his sins does not prosper, but whoever confesses and renounces them finds mercy." In 1 John 1:8-9 we read, "If we claim to be without sin, we deceive ourselves and the truth is not in us. If we confess our sins, he is faithful and just and will forgive us our sins and purify us from all unrighteousness."

Unfortunately, I wasn't willing to see the sinful anger at work in my heart. I knew I had a quick temper, but I unrealistically thought

I had it under control. The truth was I did a lot of foolish things and I said a lot of hurtful things when I lost control and got angry. Proverbs 14:17 says, "A quick-tempered man does foolish things." Even though I couldn't see it, I was acting foolishly because of my temper and with time things only got worse. Finally, I reached the place my anger showed up all the time. Any little thing would set me off. When someone said or did something to me that I didn't like, I'd strike out immediately or I would hold those things in and eventually get even. I couldn't just let things go. Instead, I became revengeful and argumentative, using sharp and painful words or physical violence to hurt others. Still, I continued to say I didn't have a problem with anger.

What about you? Are you saying the same thing I used to say? Are you ashamed to acknowledge you have a problem? Do you find yourself blaming others for your anger rather than owning up to your own responsibility in the matter? What will it take for you to face reality? Don't wait as long as I did and end up imprisoned by your anger. Now is the time to turn things around.

A second way of thinking that will prevent you from dealing with your anger is believing there is no way you can change.

When I finally reached the place I could no longer deny I was the angry young man others were saying I was, I began to say I couldn't change because that was just the way I was. When others tried to talk to me about my anger, I'd tell them this was who I was, and if they didn't like it, they didn't have to talk to me or be around me. I liked to say I couldn't help who I was and I couldn't change. In fact, I took pride in what I was doing. I know now how very foolish that attitude was. Proverbs 10:23 says, "A fool finds pleasure in evil conduct." All my attitude did was make me foolishly stay exactly the way I was.

What about you? Have you told yourself the same lie I told myself? Do you think you can't change? Are you convinced you will always be the way you are now? I want to tell you that you can change, but not by yourself. You've probably already tried to turn things around at some point and failed. Maybe you've even tried dealing with your anger time and time again and always failed. If so, I have some good news for you. The Lord Jesus Christ can and will do what you can't do on your own. Jesus says in Mark 10:27, "With man this is impossible, but not with God; all things are possible with God." And the prophet Jeremiah says in Jeremiah 32:17, "Ah, Sovereign Lord, you have made the heavens and the earth by your great power and outstretched arm. Nothing is too hard for you."

You may be asking in your mind and heart whether God can really change the mess you've made of your life because of your attitude and actions. The answer is yes. Paul says in Philippians 1:6, "Being confident of this, that he who began a good work in you will carry it on to completion until the day of Christ Jesus." Paul also says in Philippians 2:13, "[Not in your own strength] for it is God Who is all the while effectually at work in you [energizing and creating in you the power and desire], both to will and to work for His good pleasure *and* satisfaction *and* delight." (Amplified Bible)

Think about it and take the time to complete this book before you decide there's no way you can change. The Lord Jesus Christ is waiting to empower you to do what you can't do yourself. Scripture puts it this way: "I have strength for all things in Christ Who empowers me. [I am ready for anything and equal to anything through Him Who infuses inner strength into me; I am self-sufficient in Christ's sufficiency]. Philippians 4:13 (Amplified Bible)

God understands your struggles and the attitudes of your heart better than anyone else. Why not give Him a chance to deal with your anger and turn things around for you?

TALKING TO GOD BEFORE YOU BEGIN

Father God, be with me as I study this book. Enable me to be honest with myself and to take responsibility for my anger and my actions. Bring me to the place I can confess I have a problem with anger and forgive me for believing the lie that I can not change. Teach me to control my anger before it destroys me, my family, and my future. AMEN

If you are feeling afraid right now about confronting your anger or if you found it difficult to pray this prayer, it's OK. Don't give up on the book or put it down; take a chance and read on. You won't be sorry you did.

Part I
Five Attitudes That Set Off Anger

Everybody gets angry or upset. It's not getting angry that's the problem; it's how you express those feelings of anger that determines whether you are sinning or not. The Amplified Bible puts it this way: "When angry do not sin, do not ever let your wrath, your exasperation, your fury, or indignation last until the sun goes down. Leave no room or foothold for the devil, give no opportunity to him."
—Ephesians 4:26-27

That's not all the Bible has to say about anger. It also defines for us what anger is, why it shows up, and how it can be overcome. Not only does the Word offer a lot of helpful wisdom on recognizing and dealing with sinful anger, it includes many examples of people who struggled with anger. You and I can profit from looking at those people and seeing the consequences of anger in their lives.

I wish I had done that when I was young and just getting started with my anger; only I didn't. Instead, I took pride in my anger. I'd say, "Everybody gets angry. This is just who I am. If you don't like it, you don't have to be around me." I didn't realize at the time how harmful and destructive that attitude was. Yes, I was right when I said everyone gets angry or upset about something in life. Anger is a God-given emotion that enables us to deal with things that are displeasing and uncomfortable for us. God allows us to be angry, but does not want us to sin by holding onto our anger and letting it get out of control.

Some of you might be thinking like I used to think that it's impossible for you to avoid your anger. Or you might be thinking if you let your anger go, you'll look weak and others might take advantage of you. The truth is it takes a strong person, not a weakling, to avoid anger or control it when it does show up. Solomon says in Proverbs 14:29, "A patient man has great understanding, but a quick-tempered man displays folly."

Getting upset, developing a vengeful attitude, committing violent actions, thinking negative thoughts, becoming argumentative, raising your voice, using sharp words or cursing, as well as holding things in and refusing to let them go are all symptoms of not controlling your anger. What's more, the longer you ignore your anger and don't deal with it, the worse it will get. David tells us in Psalm 37:8: "Refrain from anger and turn from wrath; do not fret—it leads only to evil." With these words, he is warning you and me to deal with our anger because it only leads to increasing consequences.

In order to really understand what anger is and how to control it, you must first identify what is creating your anger. So let's take a look at five attitudes identified in Scripture that set off anger in your life and mine just as surely as fire ignites gasoline.

One

Rebellion

For rebellion is like the sin of divination, and arrogance like the evil of idolatry.

—1 Samuel 15:23

Nobody can tell me what to do. It's my life, and I'm gonna live it the way I want to live it. "

That was my rebellious attitude when I was growing up. Before I was even a teenager, I thought I knew what was best for me, and I didn't want anyone telling me what to do. I figured if I could get out from under my parents and the other authority figures in my life, I'd be able to do my own thing and live the way I wanted. When I looked around me at others who were living any way they chose, their lives appeared very good to me. Wanting to be just like them, I started playing hookie from school, running the streets, and breaking the law. Eventually, I found myself using drugs and robbing people in their homes and in the street. I thought this lifestyle would make me happy and untouchable; only I was wrong.

Proverbs 16:25 says, "There is a way that seems right to a man, but in the end it leads to death." 1 Corinthians 8:2 says, "The man who thinks he knows something does not yet know as he ought to know."

Of course, I had no use for the truth of Scripture back then. In my rebellion, I thought I knew it all. I know now if I had only listened to those in authority over me, my life might have been so different. If I hadn't been as rebellious and angry as I was, I'm positive I wouldn't have been in and out of training school six times before I reached the age of fifteen; I don't believe I would have had to experience the shame and embarrassment of not being able to read; I certainly don't think I would have found myself standing in front of a judge before I even turned seventeen years old receiving ten years mandatory at Parchman Penitentiary for armed robbery and attempted murder. I realize now all of these things happened to me because I had a defiant attitude which led me to think nobody could tell me what to do, and that rebellious spirit of mine almost cost me everything.

It's easy to see that the rebellion in my life produced anger, and that anger produced violence, and then that violence produced destruction in my life. We also see this pattern recorded in Scripture in the life of Cain. Genesis 4:1-13 says:

> Adam lay with his wife Eve, and she became pregnant and gave birth to Cain. She said, "With the help of the Lord I have brought forth a man." Later she gave birth to his brother Abel.

> Now Abel kept flocks, and Cain worked the soil. In the course of time Cain brought some of the fruits of the soil as an offering to the Lord. But Abel brought fat portions from some of the firstborn of his flock. The Lord looked with favor on Abel and his offering, but on Cain and his offering he did not look with favor. So Cain was very angry, and his face was downcast.

> The Lord said to Cain, "Why are you angry? Why is your face downcast? If you do what is right, will you not be accepted? But if you do not do what is right, sin is crouching at your door; it desires to have you, but you must master it."

> Now Cain said to his brother Abel, "Let's go out to the field." And while they were in the field, Cain attacked his brother Abel and killed him.

> Then the Lord said to Cain, "Where is your brother, Abel?"

"I don't know," he replied. "Am I my brother's keeper?"

The Lord said, "What have you done? Listen! Your brother's blood cries out to me from the ground. Now you are under a curse and driven from the ground, which opened its mouth to receive your brother's blood from your hand. When you work the ground, it will no longer yield its crops for you. You will be a restless wanderer on the earth."

Cain said to the Lord, "My punishment is more than I can bear."

Even though God's plan called for bringing firstfruits as a sacrifice, Cain ignored God's instructions and chose something else. Because of his rebellious choice, God didn't accept Cain's offering. On the other hand, Cain's brother Abel brought what God required when he offered the firstborn of his flock, and God accepted his offering.

Not only did Cain's rebellion lead him to disobey God, it also led him to get angry. Scripture puts it this way: "So Cain was very angry, and his face was downcast." Things didn't stop there. Even when God gave Cain a second chance to correct the problem, he didn't. Instead, Cain continued to rebel against God and allowed anger to take control. We learn this in Genesis 4:7 where it says: "The Lord said to Cain, 'Why are you angry? Why is your face downcast? If you do what is right, will you not be accepted? But if you do not do what is right, sin is crouching at your door; it desires to have you, but you must master it.'"

Cain should have listened to God; instead, he did what seemed right in his own mind, and sin slipped in and took control. In fact, his choice brought him to the place his anger led him to murder his own brother. Scripture records that event this way: "Now Cain said to his brother Abel, 'Let's go out to the field.' And while they were in the field, Cain attacked his brother Abel and killed him."

What a perfect picture of how rebellion produces anger, anger produces violence, and violence produces destruction. And this whole process could have been avoided if Cain had just ignored his rebellious desires and heeded God's instructions instead.

MAKING IT PERSONAL:

What about you? Do you have a rebellious attitude? Are you saying that it's your life and nobody can tell you what to do? Not your parents. Not your husband or wife. Not your fiancé or your boss or your teachers. Not the police. Not even God.

If so, listen to what Scripture has to say that applies to your situation:

> *The fear of the Lord is the beginning of knowledge, but fools despise wisdom and discipline.*
>
> —Proverbs 1:7

> *A fool spurns (despises) his father's discipline, but whoever heeds correction shows prudence.*
>
> —Proverbs 15:5

> *A fool finds no pleasure in understanding but delights in airing his own opinions.*
>
> —Proverbs 18:2

Would you rather be a fool or would you like to begin to deal with your rebellious refusal to heed the advice and boundaries of others? You must decide. It's up to you.

THINKING IT OVER

- Do you hate it when someone else tells you what to do?
- Do you become defensive and argumentative when somebody tries to correct or challenge you?
- Do you get angry when you can't have your way?
- Do you normally put your own feelings before the feelings of others?

If you answered yes to one or more of the questions above, you could have a rebellious spirit that is producing anger in your life. Take some time and think it over. Perhaps you might like to read the questions again and reflect on your life to get a true picture of how rebellion is affecting it. Then, you might want to begin to defuse your rebellious attitude by taking one or both of the actions steps that follow.

TAKING A POSITIVE ACTION STEP

- When someone asks you to do something in the days ahead that makes you so angry you want to resist, don't let your anger take control like you normally do. Instead, stop and ask God to help you submit. You just might be surprised at what happens!
- Identify a person or a group of people who is influencing you by encouraging you to rebel. The next time you are asked to do something rebellious, don't go along with the crowd. Instead, think of a way you can break away from them and make a better choice for yourself. If you find that hard to do, consider asking God to help you. You might want to start with the prayer below.

TALKING TO GOD

Heavenly Father, I believe I have a rebellious attitude fueling anger in my life. Give me the wisdom to see the truth about myself so I can quit fighting against the authorities and boundaries in my life. Help me not to get angry when asked or told to do something by my parents, my spouse, my teacher, my boss, or my friends. Destroy any rebellious spirit in me and enable me to submit to You and to the people in my life like I should. AMEN

HEARING FROM GOD'S WORD

In your anger do not sin; when you lie on your beds search your heart and be silent. Offer right sacrifices and trust in the Lord.
—Psalm 4:4-5

The fear of the Lord is the beginning of knowledge, but fools despise wisdom and discipline.
—Proverbs 1:7

Do not be wise in your own eyes; fear the Lord and shun evil.
—*Proverbs 3:7*

My son, keep your father's commands and do not forsake your mother's teaching. Bind them upon your heart forever; fasten them around your neck. When you walk, they will guide you; when you sleep, they will watch over you; when you awake, they will speak to you. For these commands are a lamp, this teaching is a light, and the corrections of discipline are the way to life.
—*Proverbs 6:20-23*

Honor your father and your mother, as the Lord your God has commanded you, so that you may live long and that it may go well with you.
—*Deuteronomy 5:16*

Endure hardship as discipline; God is treating you as sons. For what son is not disciplined by his father? If you are not disciplined (and everyone undergoes discipline), then you are illegitimate children and not true sons. Moreover, we have all had human fathers who disciplined us and we respected them for it. How much more should we submit to the Father of our spirits and live! Our fathers disciplined us for a little while as they thought best; but God disciplines us for our good, that we may share in his holiness. No discipline seems pleasant at the time, but painful. Later on, however, it produces a harvest of righteousness and peace for those who have been trained by it.
—*Hebrews 12:7-11*

Submit yourselves for the Lord's sake to every authority instituted among men: whether to the king, as the supreme authority, or to governors, who are sent by him to punish those who do wrong and to commend those who do right.
—*1 Peter 2:13-14*

Young men, in the same way be submissive to those who are older. All of you, clothe yourselves with humility toward one another, because, "God opposes the proud but gives grace to the humble."

Humble yourselves, therefore, under God's mighty hand, that he may lift you up in due time.

—1 Peter 5:5-6

2 Timothy 3:16 says: "All Scripture is God-breathed and useful for teaching, rebuking, correcting and training in righteousness, so that the man of God may be thoroughly equipped for every good work."

In light of this truth, you might want to seriously consider how Scriptures like those above could be helpful to you in understanding how anger is affecting your life and what you must do to get free from its control.

To help you use these Scriptures, you might want to write down one or more of them and either carry them with you or put them in a place where you can see them. Better yet, you might want to memorize them. They will help you remember the truth about how your rebellious spirit is destroying your life.

Two

Pride

Pride goes before destruction, a haughty spirit before a fall.
—*Proverbs 16:18*

Pride is the original sin and precedes all other sins. It first showed up in the Garden of Eden where it caused the downfall of Adam and Eve, and it has been plaguing mankind ever since.

When pride gets control, it takes your eyes off God and others and makes you just look at yourself. It becomes all about "me." In fact, the only thing you think about is how it makes "me" feel, how it makes "me" look, and what it can do for "me."

Pride was what Satan used to blind the eyes of Eve in the Garden of Eden as well as to persuade her to take her eyes off God and put them on herself. Genesis 3:4-6 records the event this way: "'You will not surely die,' the serpent said to the woman. 'For God knows that when you eat of it your eyes will be opened, and you will be like God, knowing good and evil.' When the woman saw that the fruit of the tree was good for food and pleasing to the eye, and also desirable for gaining wisdom, she took some and ate it. She also gave some to her husband, who was with her, and he ate it."

Once Eve had her eyes off what God had said to them about not eating from the tree and onto her own wishes, rebellion set in. Then, she persuaded Adam to join her, and they both sinned against God by eating the fruit from the tree. When they ate, the fall of man occurred and destruction followed.

Pride was also what caused Satan to destroy himself. This is recorded in Isaiah 14:12-13. It says: "How you have fallen from heaven, O morning star, son of the dawn! You have been cast down to the earth, you who once laid low the nations! You said in your heart, 'I will ascend to heaven. I will raise my throne above the stars of God; I will sit enthroned on the mount of assembly, on the utmost heights of the sacred mountain. I will ascend above the tops of the clouds; I will make myself like the Most High.' But you are brought down to the grave, to the depths of the pit."

When I was growing up, my pride kept leading me toward destruction. Because I was so angry, it didn't take much to make me mad. If someone did one thing I didn't like or said one thing I didn't agree with, I'd lose my temper. In fact, there were a lot of times when I'd get furious for no good reason at all. Once I did, I'd strike out and hurt someone or get into some kind of trouble. Sometimes I would physically attack the person who'd gotten in my way; other times I'd steal things; still other times I would destroy somebody's property. Then, when I got caught, I wouldn't admit I was wrong or ask anyone to forgive me. My pride wouldn't let me. I thought if I apologized I was being weak. As a result, I stayed in trouble with everybody from my teachers to my parents to the local police. Ultimately, my attitude of pride destroyed a lot of relationships, even some with people who loved me and were concerned about me and my future.

I've heard it said that temper gets people into trouble, but pride keeps them there. This was certainly the case for me. It was bad enough that my hot temper was always showing up, but my prideful refusal to own up to it was what actually kept me stuck in the cycles of anger and violence leaving me alone and in constant trouble.

MAKING IT PERSONAL

What about you? Is anger controlling you, but pride won't let you admit your anger is out of control? Are others telling you that you need to get your bad temper under control before you hurt someone, but you think they have a problem, not you? What will it take for you to stop letting your pride blind you concerning your anger? Do you have to destroy yourself, your family, and others in your life before you realize you need to deal with your anger?

THINKING IT OVER

- Do you hate to admit you're wrong?
- Do you think you will look weak if you back down from a confrontation?
- Are there people you've hurt, but your pride and ego won't let you apologize to them?
- Do you see areas of your life falling apart, but you are too full of pride to ask for help?

If you answered yes to one or more of the above questions, you probably have a problem with pride. In light of that, consider taking one or both of the action steps that follow. Then make your pride a matter for prayer using the short prayer at the end of this section.

TAKING A POSITIVE ACTION STEP

- Think back to the last time you hurt someone's feelings and consider how you would feel if someone had said or done those same things to you. Then ask God to show you how you could have handled the situation differently. Look for a chance to put what you've learned into practice.
- Put aside your pride and go back to a person or persons whose feelings you've hurt in the past and ask for forgiveness. Try to do this face to face if you can; but if not, it's OK for now to do it over the phone or in a note.

TALKING TO GOD

Heavenly Father, I admit I'm proud. I realize pride has interfered with my relationship with You and with others. Teach me, Lord God, how not to let my ego destroy my life, my family, and my future. Show me how to be humble and then give me the grace to live that way. Father, You say if I will humble myself under Your mighty hand, You will lift me up in due time. I ask You to do that in my life. In the name of Jesus. AMEN.

HEARING GOD'S WORD

If anyone thinks he is something when he is nothing, he deceives himself.

—Galatians 6:3

Refrain from anger and turn from wrath; do not fret—it leads only to evil.

—Psalms 37:8

Pride goes before destruction, and a haughty spirit before a fall.
—Proverbs 16:18

Pride only breeds quarrels, but wisdom is found in those who take advice.

—Proverbs 13:10

Before his downfall a man's heart is proud, but humility comes before honor.

—Proverbs 18:12

A man's pride brings him low, but a man of lowly spirit gains honor.

—Proverbs 29:23

He (God) mocks proud mockers but gives grace to the humble.
—Proverbs 3:34

God opposes the proud, but gives grace to the humble.

—James 4:6

Look back over these Scriptures and jot down or mark the ones you think apply to your own situation. You might consider memorizing one of them so that it will be always available to you when you need it. Remember that the truth of God's Word has the power to impact your life in incredible ways.

Three

Jealousy

Anger is cruel and fury overwhelming, but who can stand before jealousy?

—Proverbs 27:4

The Bible asks a question in Proverbs 27:4 you and I should really think about. That question is: "Who can stand before jealousy?"

Many people underestimate the evil power of jealousy and don't understand exactly how low it can take you. The truth is, jealousy will make you do things to other people you never imagined you would do. Remember what happened to Cain. I'm sure he never thought he'd be capable of murdering his own brother, but once he was overtaken by a spirit of jealousy, he found himself doing just that.

There is another great example in Scripture of how low jealousy will take you. Genesis 37:3-4 tells us about this situation which involved Joseph and his brothers. Listen to what happened: "Now Israel loved Joseph more than any of his other sons, because he had been born to him in his old age; and he made a richly ornamented robe for him. When his brothers saw that their father loved him more than any of them, they hated him and could not speak a kind word to him."

Genesis 37:18-20 goes on to tell us what the consequences of his brother's hatred for Joseph were. It says: "But they saw him (Joseph) in the distance, and before he reached them, they plotted to kill him. 'Here comes that dreamer!' they said to each other. 'Come now, let's kill him and throw him into one of these cisterns and say that a ferocious animal devoured him. Then we'll see what comes of his dreams.'"

Scripture goes on to say that God used Judah to intervene on Joseph's behalf convincing his brothers not to kill Joseph, but instead to sell him as a slave to the Egyptians. After they did that, they took Joseph's robe, dipped it in goat's blood, took it to their father, and told him Joseph was killed by an animal. All of this took place simply because they were jealous of their younger brother.

Back when I was the little boy who stayed in trouble at school and with the law, people used to ask me, "Eddie, why are you mad with the world? What makes you so angry and violent?" At the time I didn't know the answer to those questions, but looking back, I realize one of the reasons I acted the way I did toward other people was that I was jealous.

My family lived in poverty. We weren't just your ordinary poor; we were a notch lower. "Po" would be how some people might describe our standard of living. It seemed like I couldn't help but become outraged inside the dilapidated shot-gun house my family lived in with its rusted tin roof and sagging front porch. There was no running water indoors and the toilet was outside. There wasn't even any air conditioning. Things were very crowded with all of us all jammed up in that small, little three-room house. Usually all we had to wear were hand-me-down clothes. Not just second-hand clothes; we often wore third-hand clothes. First they belonged to somebody white, who passed them on to somebody black, who wore the clothes themselves, and instead of throwing them away, gave them to us. I hated having to wear hand-me-down clothes, but I despised it even more when I got made fun of for wearing them. I found myself asking why others around me had nice things and

I didn't. When I did, I'd get jealous, and those feelings of jealousy made me so mad I'd lash out and try to get even. When I did, all people saw was my anger; what they couldn't see was the jealousy fueling my anger.

I didn't realize it at the time, but jealousy was also blinding me from seeing who I was and keeping me from recognizing my potential. I was too busy looking at what others had or who they were to focus on what I had and who I was. As a result, those feelings of jealousy developed into an inferiority complex. I found myself hating others I thought had things or talents I didn't have so much that I wanted to hurt them any way I could.

Once I'd become jealous, I found it almost impossible to stop being envious. I've heard it said that overcoming envy is like running into the ocean—the deeper you go in the water, the harder it is to get out. I certainly found this to be true in my own life. I couldn't stop being jealous and, as a result, I couldn't deal with my anger either.

MAKING IT PERSONAL

What about you? Is your life being affected by jealousy? Has envy blinded you to the point you can't see who you are and the potential you have? You will never be able to be all God desires you to be until you stop being jealous of others. If you don't stop looking at what others have and what you don't have, you will spend all your time tearing others down, instead of spending that time and energy becoming what God has created you to be.

THINKING IT OVER

- Do you get upset when you see others being promoted while you're not?
- Do you find it easy to try to tear down the confidence and reputation of others?
- Is it difficult for you to praise others and show them appreciation?
- Do you compare yourself to others a lot?

If so, jealousy may be eating away at your heart and creating anger toward other people. However, don't be discouraged. There are ways you can deal with your jealousy. It could start as you begin to take one of the action steps that follow or as you pray the prayer that also follows.

TAKING A POSITIVE ACTION STEP

- Think of someone in your life you often tear down. As soon as you can, go to that person and pay them a compliment instead.
- The next time you find yourself feeling jealous of somebody or tearing them down by saying negative things about them, stop right where you are and tell God what you are doing is wrong. Ask Him to enable you to let it go. End the prayer by finding something positive to give thanks to God for about that particular person.

TALKING TO GOD

Heavenly Father, I admit I am jealous of others. I ask You to forgive me for the hurt and pain I've caused other people as well as for the hurtful things I've said about them. Change any negative attitudes I have about myself or others that cause me to feel the way I do. Teach me to rejoice when You bless others and to be grateful for the things You have blessed me with. Set me free from jealousy, envy, and selfish ambition, and I will thank You for it in the name of Jesus. AMEN.

HEARING GOD'S WORD

Anger is cruel and fury overwhelming, but who can stand before jealousy?

—Proverbs 27:4

A heart at peace gives life to the body, but envy rots the bones.

—Proverbs 14:30

Let us not become conceited, provoking and envying each other.
—Galatians 5:26

At one time we too were foolish, disobedient, deceived and enslaved by all kinds of passions and pleasures. We lived in malice and envy, being hated and hating one another. But when the kindness and love of God our Savior appeared, he saved us, not because of righteous things we had done, but because of his mercy. He saved us through the washing of rebirth and renewal by the Holy Spirit, whom he poured out on us generously through Jesus Christ our Savior, so that, having been justified by his grace, we might become heirs having the hope of eternal life.
—Titus 3:3-7

But if you harbor bitter envy and selfish ambition in your hearts, do not boast about it or deny the truth. Such "wisdom" does not come down from heaven but is earthly, unspiritual, of the devil. For where you have envy and selfish ambition, there you find disorder and every evil practice.
—James 3:14-16

Therefore, rid yourselves of all malice and all deceit, hypocrisy, envy, and slander of every kind.
—1 Peter 2:1

Don't overlook reading and heeding these verses from Scripture. God's Word has the power to impact your life like nothing else can. If you doubt this is true, just give it a try anyway and see what happens.

Four
Unforgiveness

*"In your anger do not sin": Do not let the sun go down while you
are still angry, and do not give the devil a foothold.*
— *Ephesians 4:26-27*

Whenever I got angry when I was growing up, my heart and mind would become a storehouse where I shut up every hurt, every offense, and every painful word someone had spoken to me or about me. Then, I'd leave those things stored in there until I got revenge. I lived by the motto, "An eye for an eye and a tooth for a tooth." If somebody did something to me, I was going to do something even worse back to them. I thought if I forgave somebody who'd hurt me, I was being weak. Only I was wrong. All my lack of forgiveness did was simply make the situation worse.

What I didn't realize back then was my failure to forgive and the anger it produced were a lot like buttermilk—the longer they sat, the more sour they became. Over time, I grew bitter from all the anger I had stored up inside of me, and that bitterness acted just like acid eating away at my life and breaking down my relationships with others.

If there was ever someone with a reason not to forgive, it was Joseph. After his brothers sold him into slavery, a lot of years passed and a lot happened in Joseph's life while he grew to be a man in Egypt. His brothers didn't know about any of this. They actually thought he was long gone and they would never see him again, but a time came when there was a great famine and all the countries had to come to Egypt to buy food. Joseph's father, Jacob, sent his ten sons there to do that. What they didn't know was their brother, Joseph, was the person in charge of the food. God had raised him up from a slave to become the second in command in Egypt. Take the time to read Genesis 37-50 to see the details of how this happened. I think you'll be blessed if you do.

When Joseph's brothers showed up to buy food for their people, Joseph immediately recognized who they were. At that moment, Joseph could have expressed hatred for his brothers; he could have repaid them for all the pain and hurt they had caused in his life; he could even have used his power to have them killed. In fact, most people would say any of those actions would have been justified. Because of his relationship with God, however, Joseph did not allow resentment, lack of forgiveness, or retaliation to fill his heart. Instead, Joseph forgave his brothers.

Genesis 45:1-7 puts it this way: "Then Joseph could no longer control himself before all his attendants, and he cried out, 'Have everyone leave my presence.' So there was no one with Joseph when he made himself known to his brothers. And he wept so loudly that the Egyptians heard him, and Pharaoh's household heard about it. Joseph said to his brothers, 'I am Joseph! Is my father still living?' But his brothers were not able to answer him, because they were terrified at his presence. Then Joseph said to his brothers, 'Come close to me.' When they had done so, he said, 'I am your brother Joseph, the one you sold into Egypt! And now, do not be distressed and do not be angry with yourselves for selling me here, because it was to save lives that God sent me ahead of you. For two years now there has been famine in the land, and for the next five years there will not be plowing and reaping. But God sent me ahead of you to preserve for you a remnant on earth and to save your lives by a great deliverance.'"

What a great picture Joseph provides us with of the power of forgiveness. Imagine how different his life and the lives of his brothers would have been if Joseph had been unforgiving and taken his revenge instead of forgiving.

MAKING IT PERSONAL

What about you? Are you willing to forgive those who've hurt you or would you rather get even? Do you live by the same motto I used to live by: "An eye for an eye and a tooth for a tooth"? Is your heart a storehouse for things others have done or said to you which have wounded you? Do you find yourself thinking if anybody does something hurtful to you, you'll do something even worse to them?

If so, you may not be able to let go of the hurt and pain others have caused you. You must keep in mind that lack of forgiveness produces anger which will eventually grow into bitterness and eat away at your life and your relationships with others. Consider the questions that follow to help you determine if you have a problem with lack of forgiveness.

THINKING IT OVER

- Do you compare yourself to others a lot?
- Is there anybody you hate being around because they remind you of the hurt and anger from the past?
- Do you find it easier to suppress your anger and hurts rather than express them?
- Are there mistakes and/or bad decisions you've made that you just can't let go of easily?

If you recognize you have a problem with forgiving, be sure to take one or both of the actions steps that follow as well as talking to God about your situation. And don't forget to listen to what God has to say to you from His Word.

47

TAKING A POSITIVE ACTION STEP

- Pick out one particular person who's hurt you in the past and then pray for that person. If you are unable to do that, consider why you can't, and then ask God to give you the grace to be able to pray for them.
- Think of someone you need to forgive, but haven't. Don't put it off any longer. Before the sun sets, either give them a call or go see them to tell them you are letting go of the hurts of the past. In addition, it would be good for you to ask them to forgive you for the ways in which you have hurt them as well.

TALKING TO GOD

Heavenly Father, teach me to forgive others. You say in Scripture that in order to be forgiven, I must be willing to forgive others. Father, I want You to be able to forgive me, so teach me to forgive those who've hurt me or made me angry. Provide me with the power to let go of any bitterness, resentment, envy, strife, and unkindness I have in my heart. I ask this in the name of the Lord Jesus Christ. AMEN

HEARING GOD'S WORD

Do not repay anyone evil for evil.

—*Romans 12:17*

Do not be overcome by evil, but overcome evil with good.
—*Romans 12:21*

Do not repay evil with evil or insult with insult.
—*1 Peter 3:9*

A man's wisdom gives him patience; it is to his glory to overlook an offense.

—*Proverbs 19:11*

For if you forgive men when they sin against you, your heavenly Father will also forgive you. But if you do not forgive men their sins, your Father will not forgive your sins.

—Matthew 6:14-15

And when you stand praying, if you hold anything against anyone, forgive him, so that your Father in heaven may forgive you your sins.

—Mark 11:25

Do not repay evil for evil. Be careful to do what is right in the eyes of everybody. If it is possible, as far as it depends on you, live at peace with everyone. Do not take revenge, my friends, but leave room for God's wrath, for it is written: "It is mine to avenge; I will repay," says the Lord.

—Romans 12:17-20

Bear with each other and forgive whatever grievances you may have against one another. Forgive as the Lord forgave you. And over all these virtues put on love, which binds them all together in perfect unity.

—Colossians 3:13-14

Get rid of all bitterness, rage and anger, brawling and slander, along with every form of malice. Be kind to one another, and compassionate to one another, forgiving each other, just as in Christ God forgave you.

—Ephesians 4:31-32

Forgiveness is pivotal to making life work like God would have it work. Take the time to meditate on these Scriptures so you can understand more clearly how you can give forgiveness to others as well as how you can receive it yourself.

Five

Fear

Fear of man will prove to be a snare, but whoever trusts in the Lord is kept safe.

—Proverbs 29:25

Not only was Joseph willing to forgive his brothers for the evil they had done to him, he actually saw his being sold into Egypt as the divine will of God to save the children of Israel from being destroyed by the famine. Still, his brothers could not believe Joseph could possibly forgive them for the hurt and pain they'd caused him. They lived in fear that once their father died Joseph would try to take revenge for what they had done to him when he was a boy. Because of the work God had done in his life, however, Joseph did not have revenge on his mind. His brothers, on the other hand, were blinded by fear and could not see or understand what was really going on with Joseph.

Listen to how their fears tormented Joseph's brothers from Genesis 50:15-21:

> When Joseph's brothers saw that their father was dead, they said, "What if Joseph holds a grudge against us and pays us back for all the wrongs we did to him?" So they sent word to Joseph, saying, "Your father left these instructions before he died: This is what you are to

say to Joseph: I ask you to forgive your brothers the sins and the wrongs they committed in treating you so badly. Now please forgive the sins of the servants of the God of your father." When their message came to him, Joseph wept. His brothers then came and threw themselves down before him. "We are your slaves," they said. But Joseph said to them, "Don't be afraid. Am I in the place of God? You intended to harm me, but God intended it for good to accomplish what is now being done, the saving of many lives. So then, don't be afraid. I will provide for you and your children." And he reassured them and spoke kindly to them.

Fear like that experienced by Joseph's brothers is a terrible thing. It often blinds you and me to the truth and keeps us in bondage to behaviors designed to protect us or give us a false sense of control. Over time, these fears often produce anger in our lives.

All my life, I've been plagued by fears. People who knew me during the years I was running the streets probably looked at my life and said there was no way this was true. In fact, it probably appeared to most folks that I was fearless. The truth, however, was I did a lot of the foolish things I did simply to hide my fears.

My biggest fear was ending up a failure. When I looked around me when I was growing up, all I saw was hopelessness. The only future in the Mississippi Delta in the 1970's for folks like me lay in farm work or house work or gin work, and those jobs only keep people poor, broke, powerless, and living at other people's mercy. Trapped in that reality, I couldn't see any chance to make something of my life. So, I turned to all I knew to do and began to try to build a reputation through crime and violence. I thought that was how I would get people to respect me. However, my choice backfired on me. As my reputation for getting into trouble grew, people began to say I would never amount to anything. When I started to hear those words, I became overwhelmed by an even greater fear of failure, and that led to even more fear-driven anger and violence.

My fears didn't stop there, however. I also thought no one loved me, not even God. For most of my life, my own father rejected me. All my growing up years, he never once told me he loved me. Not once. What's more, he beat me on a regular basis. My father wasn't the only one rejecting me, however. As I became more angry and violent, other people around me began to fear me and keep their distance. As a result, I figured I was worthless. It seemed to me I couldn't do anything right. On top of it all, I did so poorly in school I thought I was dumb and didn't have any talents at all.

Because I didn't know how to deal with my fears, I tried to run from them, only I couldn't. Wherever I went, all those fears were still there. As a result, I became more and more angry and more and more violent. Eventually, my main goal in life became to hurt other people before they hurt me in order to protect myself from all my worst fears coming true.

MAKING IT PERSONAL

What about you? Do you have fears of your own that are tormenting you? Do you know that the more you run from your fears, the stronger they will get? You see, Satan knows if he can keep you running, he will have control over you. You must keep in mind that Satan is the tormentor and he wants to rob you of every good thing God wants to give to you. So, Satan uses fear to keep you locked up so you can't enjoy the freedom you have in the Lord Jesus Christ. Jesus says in John 10:10, "The thief comes only to steal and kill and destroy; I have come that they may have life, and have it to the full." I want to ask you a question. It may sound like a dumb question, but I want you to think about it anyway. The question is: If a thief and a murderer showed up at your door, would you let him in? You are probably thinking there is no way you would do that knowing he was going to steal from you or try to hurt you or maybe even kill you. But, consider this: Fear is that thief and murderer who shows up at the door of your mind and heart looking to destroy you. Have you let fear into your life? If you have, then you have let in a thief!

THINKING IT OVER

- Are you afraid to open up and show love to people? If so, why?

- Do you expect others only to hurt and disappoint you?
- Do you find it hard not to be defensive and guarded in a relationship?
- Are there things in your past you are ashamed of and afraid someone will find out?

Consider your answers to these questions. Do they indicate you have fears in your life that are creating anger? If so, you might need to address your fears so you can begin to deal with the anger they promote. You could start that process by taking the action step below and praying the prayer that follows.

TAKING A POSITIVE ACTION STEP

- Pick two people you love but are afraid to tell you do. Go to them and say "I love you." If you aren't able to say it out loud right now, think of a way you can show them your love. A hug or a kiss or a compliment or a helping hand might be a great way to do this.
- Ask God to show you someone you can talk to about your fears. Get together with that person as soon as possible and share as honestly as you can about those fears. It would be great if you would ask them to pray for you. If you can't find someone to talk to about your fears, spend some extended time reflecting on the Scriptures listed here, asking God to reveal to you what your fears are and how they can be overcome.

TALKING TO GOD

Heavenly Father, I ask You to give me the power to overcome the fears plaguing my life, and to set me free from any hidden fears buried deep inside me. I realize my fears are making me defensive and keeping me away from people I think might hurt me or take advantage of me. As a result, my behavior is destroying my relationships with others. You tell us in Your Word that You don't give us a spirit of fear, but instead offer us love, power, and peace. Father, fill my heart with

Your love, power, and peace so my life will no longer be consumed with fear. In Jesus' name. AMEN.

HEARING GOD'S WORD

For God has not given us the spirit of fear, but of power and of love and of a sound mind.
—2 Timothy 1:7

There is no fear in love. But perfect love drives out fear, because fear has to do with punishment. The one who fears is not made perfect in love. We love God because He first loved us.
—1 John 4:18-19

The thief comes only to steal and to kill and to destroy; I have come that they may have life, and have it to the full.
—John 10:10

Be self-controlled and alert. Your enemy the devil prowls around like a roaring lion, looking for someone to devour. Resist him, standing firm in the faith.
—1 Peter 5:8

Fear of man will prove to be a snare, but whoever trusts in the Lord is kept safe.
—Proverbs 29:25

Do not be anxious about anything, but in everything, by prayer and petition, with thanksgiving, present your requests to God. And the peace of God, which transcends all understanding will guard your hearts and your minds in Christ Jesus.
—Philippians 4:6-7

Fight your fears with the truth of the Word. Write down or memorize one of these verses and read or quote it the next time you feel afraid or defeated; then be prepared to watch your fears fade away. Does that sound too good to be true? Give it a try. It really does work!

Part II
Eight Negative Effects Of Uncontrolled Anger

Now that you've considered some of the attitudes igniting your anger, let's take a look at eight negative effects of uncontrolled anger and how they might be at work in your life. These eight attitudes are identified in Scripture. In fact, all of them are found in the Genesis 4:1-13, which is the account of Cain and Abel we've already talked about. If you haven't done it yet, read this complete section of Scripture. As you do, open your heart and your mind and let the Word of God speak to you. Then, stay receptive to the truth of God's Word as you work your way through this section of the book.

One

Anger Hinders Your Ability to Listen

*Then the Lord said to Cain, "Why are you angry? Why is your face
downcast? If you do what is right, will you not be accepted? But if
you do not do what is right, sin is crouching at your door; it desires
to have you, but you must master it."*

—Genesis 4:6-7

You will remember that Cain made the choice to offer a
sacrifice to God that was not acceptable by bringing what
he chose, not what God had chosen. Cain's brother Abel,
on the other hand, obeyed the Lord and brought him the best—the
firstborn—as God had asked. Consequently, God accepted Abel's
offering, but not Cain's. This made Cain very angry.

Why, you might be asking, was Cain angry? The answer is
simple. Rebellion creates anger, and Cain was obviously in rebellion
against God's requirements which produced his anger. In fact, Cain
was so angry that when God spoke to him about his problem, Cain
could not hear a word God said to him. Not only that, even when
God showed Cain the solution to his problem by telling him if he
would do what was right he would be accepted, Cain still didn't
hear or obey. Instead, Cain began to blame someone else rather
than taking responsibility for his own problem, and that kind of
thinking led him to even more drastic behavior.

I think God was hoping Cain would listen to His words and realize how serious his rebellion and anger were. Remember what the Lord said to Cain:

"'Why are you angry? Why is your face downcast? If you do what is right, will you not be accepted? But if you do not do what is right, sin is crouching at your door; it desires to have you, but you must master it.'"

If God were to say those same words to me and you today, would we take heed or would we ignore God's words just like Cain did? I don't know about you, but there have been so many times in my life when if I had only have listened to what God or other people were saying to me, it would have saved me a lot of trouble and possibly someone else a lot of pain. Instead, I often found myself responding just like Cain did.

As a young man, I would just shut down emotionally when I was angry. When people tried to talk to me, I couldn't hear a word they were saying. My ears and my mind would just tune them out. Instead, I'd focus on my anger. Often the words someone was trying to say to me only inflamed the situation even more. In fact, a lot of the time, the more they tried to talk to me, the angrier I got.

The Bible says in James 1:19-20, "My dear brothers, take note of this: Everyone should be quick to listen, slow to speak, and slow to become angry, for man's anger does not bring about the righteous life that God desires."

These words speak directly to who I was a young man. Back then, I was quick to speak and to become angry, but I was always slow to listen. Consequently, I said and did things that created troublesome situations for me which could have been avoided if only I had been willing to listen to the advice of others.

MAKING IT PERSONAL

What about you? How many times have you had someone say to you, "Why didn't you listen to me?" Or maybe people are always telling you, "You didn't hear a word I said." In spite of knowing they are right, do you just get mad and lose control? Is it possible anger is dulling your hearing? If so, you may have a serious problem. Think about it by asking yourself the questions that follow.

THINKING IT OVER

- Are you hard to talk to when you get upset?
- Do you withdraw when you feel angry or threatened?
- Do you find yourself shutting down emotionally when you get angry?
- When you get mad, do you only focus on your own hurt and anger and forget all about other people's hurt and pain?

If you sense you are withdrawing and failing to listen because of anger, there is hope to change the situation. Begin to listen to God as you try to take one of the action steps that follow, pray the prayer included here, and study what God's Word has to say about the matter.

TAKING A POSITIVE ACTION STEP

- The next time someone says to you that you are not listening to them, don't just blow them off. Instead, agree with them that you are not listening, ask for forgiveness, and then give them another chance to finish saying what is on their mind.
- One day this week, initiate a conversation with someone you are in relationship with—maybe your mother or father, your brother or sister, your wife or husband, your neighbor or co-worker—about something you would ordinarily find difficult to talk about with them. If the conversation starts to make you uncomfortable or angry, don't leave or stop talking. Try to hang in there and see what happens. You may need to ask God to enable you to stick around and deal with the situation properly by continuing the conversation. If you can do that, perhaps you just might be able to get a new perspective on the subject.

TALKING TO GOD

Lord, teach me to listen. I know sometimes I rush to conclusions before I hear the whole matter, and I'm aware of the fact that I often fail to be sensitive to other people's feelings. You've told me, Lord, in Scripture that I should be quick to listen, slow to speak, and slow to become angry. I realize I need help to do this. I ask You not to allow my anger to stop me from listening to You and to others. I ask this in the name of the Lord Jesus Christ. AMEN.

HEARING GOD'S WORD

My dear brothers, take note of this: Everyone should be quick to listen, slow to speak and slow to become angry, for man's anger does not bring about the righteous life that God desires.

—*James 1:19*

Go near to listen rather than to offer the sacrifice of fools, who do not know that they do wrong.

—*Ecclesiastes 5:1*

Two

Anger Changes Your Physical Appearance and Expression

Then the Lord said to Cain, "Why are you angry? Why is your face downcast?"

—*Genesis 4:6*

When God asked Cain why his face was downcast, I believe God was actually saying to him, "I can see by the look on your face that you are angry and unhappy." That's because sooner or later anger shows up on our face and affects our physical expression. As angry as Cain was, it was surely obvious to those around him, especially God.

I want you to think about the last time you got angry. It may have been today; it might have been yesterday; perhaps it was last week. Whenever it was, think about how you looked. Did you react like a bull pounding and scratching the ground ready to charge with your nostrils flaring, your mouth pursing, your eyes squinting and your face distorted? Did you raise your voice, tighten your jaw, clinch your fist, or get red in the face? Perhaps you experienced a nervous twitch. Or maybe your body began to shake, or you felt anxious or restless. Even if you were not aware of these physical manifestations of anger, those around you probably were and it most likely affected how they felt about their relationship with you.

What's more, when you reach the point where there are symptoms of anger in your body, your anger is not just harmful to others, it is also having a damaging effect on your own health—both physical and emotional.

Dr. Carole D. Stovall, a Washington, DC, psychologist says, "Over time, unchecked anger carries a host of consequences. High blood pressure, cardiovascular disorders and heart disease, aggravation to diabetes, kidney malfunctions, urinary problems, weakened immune system, digestive disorders, prolonged headaches, and even cancer are among the health problems associated with chronic anger."

When we get angry, Dr. Neil Clark Warren says, "Our heart beats faster, our blood pressure increases, adrenaline is secreted more rapidly, more sugar is released into our system, our muscles tense, and our external arteries constrict." He also says, "When you see these signs they are troubling and threatening, in need of immediate attention."

Even if there are not internal physical manifestations of anger, there will always be the outward emotional symptoms. Others will be able to see how your anger is driving you to irrational behavior and they will be uncomfortable being around you. Anger that goes on for long periods of time can also lead to depression and possibly suicidal thoughts or actions.

For me, there came a day when my anger drove me to try to take my own life. It happened when I was in solitary confinement in the Washington County Jail in 1979. I was so depressed, so emotionally strung out, so distraught that I took a whole handful of pills. I'm not sure I really wanted to die, but I was so despondent I was willing to take that chance. As it turned out, I didn't die, but I also didn't really get the help I was desperately crying out for by overdosing. So, I remained just as angry as I always had been, at least until Jesus Christ turned my life around a few years down the road.

MAKING IT PERSONAL

What about you? Are you experiencing ills in your body and don't know why? Have you been to the doctor a lot lately, but are not getting well? I encourage you to check your heart and see if there is any unresolved anger there. Keep in mind that anger is like acid in our bodies; it can eat away at our health unless we deal with it.

God wants us to be healthy and enjoy a long and prosperous life. 3 John 2 says, "Dear friend, I pray that you may enjoy good health and that all may go well with you, even as your soul is getting along well."

The reason God wants us to be healthy is that if we belong to him our bodies are the dwelling place for God. Paul tells us in 1 Corinthians 3:16, "Don't you know that you yourselves are God's temple and that God's Spirit lives in you?" Paul also tells us in 1 Corinthians 6:19-20, "Do you not know that your body is a temple of the Holy Spirit, who is in you, whom you have received from God? You are not your own; you were bought at a price. Therefore honor God with your body."

THINKING IT OVER

- Have others begun to notice that you always have a mad or a sad look on your face?
- Are you afraid to laugh? Have you lost your smile?
- Do you find yourself easily depressed?
- Are you experiencing physical illness and don't know why?
- Have you ever considered or tried taking your own life?

Then, it could be that your anger has reached the point it is affecting your emotional and physical health. You might want to consider what the ultimate cost will be for you and decide to change the situation before it gets the best of you.

TAKING A POSITIVE ACTION STEP

- Do an attitude check on yourself by taking a long hard look at yourself in the biggest mirror you can find. See if you can give yourself a smile. If all you can muster up is a frown or a sneer, it may mean you are overcome with anger. Don't leave the mirror defeated. Stick around until a smile breaks through. Or come back again tomorrow or the next day and see what happens.
- Ask someone you trust to honestly evaluate your physical appearance. If you need to, ask them straight out if they notice anger on your face, in your speech, or in your body language. If you are open to it, ask them to keep you accountable for your appearance until it has changed. Remember this kind of change will only come from the inside out.
- If you have been experiencing physical symptoms that could be related to anger, like headaches, heartburn, depression, you should schedule a physical exam for yourself. When you get there, speak honestly with the doctor about your problems with anger and take to heart whatever medical advice is offered you.

TALKING TO GOD

Father God, I confess the anger, resentment, hostility, bitterness, and lack of forgiveness I hold in my heart for others. I find myself becoming depressed, anxious, and restless. I realize my anger is showing up on my face. I am looking mad and unhappy, and I know this is not your will for me, Lord. Show me how to let things go before they destroy me or cause me to harm myself or somebody else. I pray this in Christ's name. AMEN

HEARING GOD'S WORD

Then the Lord said to Cain, "Why are you angry? Why is your face downcast?"

—Genesis 4:6

Do not be overwicked and do not be a fool—why die before your time?

—*Ecclesiastes 7:17*

Dear friend, I pray that you may enjoy good health and that all may go well with you, even as your soul is getting along well.

—*3 John 2*

Don't you know that you yourselves are God's temple and that God's Spirit lives in you? If anyone destroys God's temple, God will destroy him; for God's temple is sacred, and you are that temple.

—*1 Corinthians 3:16-17*

Do you not know that your body is a temple of the Holy Spirit, who is in you, whom you have received from God? You are not your own; you were bought at a price. Therefore honor God with your body.

—*1 Corinthians 6:19-20*

Three

Anger Causes You to Develop a Victim Mentality

And he (God) said, "Who told you that you were naked? Have you eaten from the tree that I commanded you not to eat from?"

The man said, "The woman you put here with me—she gave me some fruit from the tree, and I ate it."

Then the Lord God said to the woman, "What is this you have done?"

The woman said, "The serpent deceived me, and I ate."
—Genesis 3:11-13

You will remember Cain developed a victim mentality when God told him he was rejecting his offering because it was not the firstfruits. Instead of taking responsibility for his choice, Cain got mad at God and then angry at his brother. Even when God gave him a second chance, Cain still maintained his victim attitude. Listen to these words God said to Cain recorded in Genesis 4:7, "'If you do what is right, will you not be accepted? But if you do not do what is right, sin is crouching at your door; it desires to have you, but you must master it.'"

How did Cain respond? Did he do what was right or did he allow sin to slip in? It would have been so easy for Cain to say to

God, "I'm sorry. Will you please forgive me?" Just those few little words would have saved him so much trouble and sorrow. Instead, his anger caused him to have a victim mentality and, instead of taking responsibility for what he'd done, he began to focus the blame for his sin on his brother.

Cain isn't the only person in the Bible who had a victim mentality. Three more come to mind. The first two were Adam and Eve. When they were confronted with their sin, they too made excuses. Listen to what Adam and Eve had to say when God confronted them in Genesis 3:9-13 about their having sinned by eating from the forbidden tree in the middle of the garden:

> But the Lord God called to the man, "Where are you?" He answered, "I heard you in the garden, but I was afraid because I was naked; so I hid." And he said, "Who told you that you were naked? Have you eaten from the tree that I commanded you not to eat from?" The man said, "The woman you put here with me—she gave me some of the fruit from the tree, and I ate it." Then the Lord God said to the woman, "What is this you have done?" The woman said, "The serpent deceived me, and I ate."

Then there was King Saul. He played the blame game as well. Here is the account of what he said when Samuel confronted him in 1 Samuel 15:19-21 about his actions which went against God's command:

> "Why did you not obey the Lord? Why did you pounce on the plunder and do evil in the eyes of the Lord?" "But I did obey the Lord," said Saul. "I went on the mission the Lord assigned me. I completely destroyed the Amalekites and brought back Agar their king. The soldiers took the sheep and cattle from the plunder, the best of what was devoted to God, in order to sacrifice them to the Lord your God at Gilgal."

Like Adam and Eve, Saul didn't take responsibility for his actions. Instead, he tried to make it sound like he had done nothing wrong but was only a victim even though that was not the truth of the situation.

Just like Cain and Adam and Eve and Saul, I had a victim mentality most of my life. I always blamed others for my actions. There were so many times when I'd say to somebody, "If you hadn't pushed me, I would not have hit you." Or "You made me say that." Or "I didn't mean to hurt you, but you made me lose it." Or "You need to stop making me mad."

As long as I was not taking responsibility for my own actions, I was never able to overcome my anger. Finally, there came the day I realized I had no one else to blame but myself. That was the day I found myself standing before a judge and hearing him say, "Eddie Spencer, if the man you beat dies, you will get the death penalty." At that moment, I realized no one had made me beat that man without mercy. I was totally responsible for the choice I'd made, and now that choice was about to send me to prison, possibly even put me on death row. For the first time in my life, the blame game didn't work! There was no one else I could point my finger at, only me.

MAKING IT PERSONAL

What about you? Are you playing the blame game? Do you make excuses for your actions rather than take responsibility for your wrong choices? If this is the case, you will never be able to control your anger; your anger will keep on controlling you. What has to happen in your life before you'll take responsibility for your own anger? For me, it took being sentenced to ten years mandatory for armed robbery and attempted murder. What will it be for you?

THINKING IT OVER

- Do you rationalize your anger a lot?
- Do you demand people apologize to you, but find it hard to say you're sorry to others yourself?
- When you're angry, do you only think about how bad you're hurting and give no thought to what anyone else might be feeling?
- When you hurt somebody, do you feel any sorrow or remorse?

TAKING A POSITIVE ACTION STEP

- Pick out a friend or acquaintance you've blamed in the past for something you were really responsible for doing or saying. Go to them and admit you were at fault, not them. This may be very difficult to do, so ask God to give you the desire and the words to carry it out.
- Think of somebody you need to apologize to for something you did or said. Go to the person and make that apology without trying to justify any of your behavior. Simply ask for forgiveness or say you're sorry and not one word more. If you are not accustomed to doing this, you may need to practice before you go to that person. Ask God to show you how to do this. Stick to the plan you practiced; otherwise, it could be so easy to begin to make excuses.

TALKING TO GOD

Lord, forgive me for blaming others for my anger. I realize I need to take responsibility for my own behavior, actions, and words. Hold me accountable for my choices and convict me when I am in denial. I ask this in Jesus' name. AMEN.

HEARING GOD'S WORD

Then the Lord said to Cain, "Where is your brother, Abel?" "I don't know," he replied. "Am I my brother's keeper?"

—Genesis 4:9

He whose walk is blameless is kept safe, but he whose ways are perverse will suddenly fall.

—Proverbs 28:18

Then the man and his wife heard the sound of the Lord God as he was walking in the garden in the cool of the day, and they hid from the Lord God among the trees of the garden. But the Lord God called to the man, "Where are you?"

He answered, "I heard you in the garden, and I was afraid because I was naked; so I hid."

And he said, "Who told you that you were naked? Have you eaten from the tree that I commanded you not to eat from?"

The man said, "The woman you put here with me—she gave me some of the fruit from the tree, and I ate it."

Then the Lord God said to the woman, "What is this you have done?"

The woman said, "The serpent deceived me and I ate."

—Genesis 3:8-13

When Samuel reached him, Saul said, "The Lord bless you! I have carried out the Lord's instruction."

But Samuel said, "What then is this bleating of sheep in my ears? What is this lowing of cattle that I hear?"

Saul answered, "The soldiers brought then from the Amalekites; they spared the best of the sheep and the cattle to sacrifice to the Lord your God, but we totally destroyed the rest."

"Stop!" Samuel said to Saul. "Let me tell what the Lord said to me last night."

"Tell me," Saul replied.

Samuel said, "Although you were once small in your own eyes, did you not become the head of the tribes of Israel? The Lord anointed you king over Israel. And he sent you on a mission, saying, "Go and completely destroy those wicked people, the Amalekites; make war on them until you have wiped them out.' Why did you not obey the Lord? Why did you pounce on the plunder and do evil in the eyes of the Lord?"

"But I did obey the Lord," Saul said. "I went on the mission the Lord assigned me. I completely destroyed the Amalekites and brought back Agag their king. The soldiers took sheep and cattle from the plunder, the best of what was devoted to God, in order to sacrifice them to the Lord your God at Gilgal."

—1 Samuel 15:13-21

If we claim to be without sin, we deceive ourselves and the truth is not in us. If we confess our sins, he is faithful and just and will forgive us our sins and purify us from all unrighteousness. If we claim we have not sinned, we make him out to be a liar and his word has no place in our lives.

—1 John 1:8-10

Four

Anger Creates a Sense of Powerlessness

"In your anger do not sin": Do not let the sun go down while you are still angry, and do not give the devil a foothold.
                                                          —Ephesians 4:26-27

ow many of these statements are you familiar with?

- "I just lost control of myself."
- "I don't know what came over me."
- "My temper simply got the best of me."
- "I don't normally act this way, but when I get angry I can't help myself!"

Proverbs 14:17 tells us that "A quick-tempered man does foolish things." And Ecclesiastes 7:9 says, "Do not be quickly provoked in your spirit, for anger resides in the lap of fools."

When you get angry and are unable to control it, anger will begin to control you. Eventually you will find yourself doing things you never thought you would do and saying things you never thought you would say. In this respect, anger is like an addiction. Once you're addicted, you lose the ability to control the situation

75

you are in, and then it isn't long before the addiction begins to destroy everything in your life.

Remember what happened to Cain. When he got angry at God, he had no idea his anger would begin to control his life. Yet, even when God gave him the opportunity to take control of his anger and correct the situation he was in, Cain didn't. Remember what the Lord asked Cain in Genesis 4:7, "If you do what is right, will you not be accepted? But if you do not do what is right, sin is crouching at your door; it desires to have you, but you must master it."

Even when God gave him a second chance, Cain let his anger dictate his decision and he did what he never thought he would do—he killed his own brother.

Just like Cain, I believe many of us underestimate the power of anger we've not dealt with in much the same way a drug addict or alcoholic underestimates the effects of the drugs or alcohol on his life. When we do, we let it go until we no longer have control over our anger, and eventually we begin to experience a sense of being powerless concerning our temper. By then, anger has a foothold in our lives, and we are entrapped in sin.

When I look back over my own life, I can see how my anger took over and controlled my life. For most of my childhood, any little thing someone said or did upset me. That progressed until I reached the place where this strong sensation would come over me when I got angry, compelling me to act out. Once that happened, I was powerless and would act on my anger no matter what.

I can think of many instances in my life when my anger got out of control, but there is one particular incident where I totally lost it. I was fourteen years old and living on Hinds Street in Greenville. I got into a confrontation with this grown man who falsely accused me of something. When he did, I picked up a two by four and tore into him. One blow with the board and he was down on the ground, out cold. The fight should have been over right then, only I didn't stop. I just kept on hitting him and hitting him and hitting him. I couldn't quit. My anger had such a hold on my mind and soul that I was absolutely over the edge. Even though I knew I was totally out of control, still I couldn't stop. I was high on my own anger.

One of the witnesses at my trial said I was behaving just like an animal. Looking back, that was true. I was so out of control it was truly a miracle I didn't beat the man to death.

MAKING IT PERSONAL

What about you? Is your anger out of control? Are you over the edge? Do you feel powerless? Do you feel you can't help losing it when you get angry?

Well, there's help for you just like there was help for me. If you want to get beyond the stronghold anger has on your life, read on and learn what can be done to change things.

THINKING IT OVER

- When you get angry, do you automatically lose control of your temper?
- When you are upset, do you feel you must let it be known no matter what?
- When you lose your temper, do you find yourself saying or doing things before you realize what you have said or done?
- Do you want to control your anger, but feel there are things you can't change that are stopping you?

TAKING A POSITIVE ACTION STEP

- The next time you get angry don't give in to your anger. As soon as you sense your emotions getting out of control, stop and ask God to keep you from giving in to your rage. Walk away from the situation if you have to, but as soon as you can, come back to the person or people involved and confess your anger to them. Ask for forgiveness and for their help in overcoming your anger. You will also need to confess your anger to God.
- Scripture has a lot to say about the power you have in Christ. Set aside some time and consider carefully the verses listed

in this section. You might also want to get a Bible and see what other verses you can find that talk about the power you have in Christ. Add them to the list in this study guide or mark them in your Bible.

TALKING TO GOD

Lord God, forgive me for allowing anger to take control over my life. It has such a hold on me that I feel a sense of being powerless when I get angry. Proverbs 14:17, "A quick tempered man does foolish things." I confess I am that person. Forgive me for giving in to my anger and give me the power to overcome it. In Jesus' name. AMEN.

HEARING FROM GOD'S WORD

Stay away from a foolish man, for you will not find knowledge on his lips.
—Proverbs 14:7

Do not be quickly provoked in your spirit, for anger resides in the lap of fools.
—Ecclesiastes 7:9

"In your anger do not sin": Do not let the sun go down while you are still angry, and do not give the devil a foothold.
—Ephesians 4:26-27

So if the Son sets you free, you will be free indeed.
—John 8:36

Five

Anger Turns to Violence

Now Cain said to his brother Abel, "Let's go out to the field." And while they were in the field, Cain attacked his brother Abel and killed him.

—Genesis 4:8

When anger takes hold and gets totally out of control, it eventually turns to violence of one kind of another. It may only make you slam the door or kick the dog, but it can also bring you to the place where you hurt somebody physically or even try to kill them. That's where it took Cain. Genesis 4:8 says, "Cain attacked his brother Abel and killed him." This happened despite the fact God warned Cain about the consequence of his anger and gave him an opportunity to turn things around.

With time, the violence produced by uncontrolled anger will become a way of life, and you will find yourself living over the edge. That's what happened to me.

In the years before I dealt with my anger, I found myself involved in many violent confrontations, but there came the day my anger went over the edge to a whole new level of rage. Here's what happened: I was locked up in the Washington County Jail. Even though I was only fifteen years old at the time, I was waiting to stand trial as an adult for armed robbery. One evening, I got into a fight with a guy who'd made me mad. Not too long after we got into it, another guy jumped in on our fight. Out of nowhere, he hit me with a stick with a nail in it. When he did, the nail caught the top of my head and blood started flowing everywhere. He hit me again, and this time the nail stuck into the flesh behind my ear drawing more blood. I could feel my anger escalating like never before. I quickly became what I would call "fire" angry. Enraged, I ran out of the cell and down to the kitchen, grabbed the biggest butcher knife I could find, and raced back to the cell where I'd been fighting with those two guys. I walked up to the man who'd hit me with the stick and grabbed him behind the head. It all happened so fast I don't think he even recognized I had a knife until I hit him in his side with it. Once I had the knife in his flesh, I jerked the guy toward me with the hand I had behind his neck and finished things off by lifting the knife up under his ribs. There was no remorse or sorrow, only a rush of power like I'd never felt before. I grew absolutely high with the excitement of what I had just done. Just like a drug, anger had taken control of my life and provided me with a rush of satisfaction that only fueled my addiction to anger and kept me enslaved to violence.

MAKING IT PERSONAL

What about you? Do you take pleasure in causing other people harm? Is violence a way of life for you? If so, I hope you will not wait until you have seriously hurt someone before you realize you are addicted and need to be set free. It's possible to be freed from your addiction to anger. I know, because it happened in my own life. The question is do you want to be set free? Read on and discover how that can happen.

THINKING IT OVER

- Is it hard for you to let things go?
- When you get angry, do you feel you must strike out?

- When someone hurts you or makes you mad, do you think you have to get revenge?
- Do you think others will see you as weak if you back down from a confrontation or a fight?

TAKING A POSITIVE ACTION STEP

- If you get angry to the point of being violent in the near future, don't act on those feelings. Instead, walk away and then thank God you were strong enough to stop.
- Make a mental list of those people you have dealt with in violent ways both in the past and in recent days. Admit you owe each of those people an apology. Decide who will be the first one you will ask to forgive you and take care of that as soon as possible. But, don't stop there. Keep on working down your list until you've asked each one of them to forgive you. Don't set a time or distance limit on this matter. Stick with it until you've spoken to all of them.

TALKING TO GOD

Father God, forgive me for all the people I've hurt because of my inability to deal with anger. I'm sorry for the pain I've caused them. Give me the power to go and apologize to those I've abused physically, mentally, emotionally, or even spiritually. Teach me how to turn away from violence altogether. I ask this in the name of Jesus. AMEN.

HEARING GOD'S WORD

Now Cain said to his brother Abel, "Let's go out to the field." And while they were in the field, Cain attacked his brother Abel and killed him.
—Genesis 4:8

Commit your way to the Lord; trust in him.
—Psalm 37:5

Jesus said, "If you hold to my teaching, you are really my disciples. Then you will know the truth and the truth will set you free."
—*John 8:31-32*

Six

Anger Destroys Your Relationships with Others

Now Cain said to his brother Abel, "Let's go out to the field." And while they were in the field, Cain attacked his brother Abel and killed him.

—Genesis 4:8

When anger takes hold and gets totally out of control, it eventually turns to violence of one kind of another. It may only make you slam the door or kick the dog, but it can also bring you to the place where you hurt somebody physically or even try to kill them. That's where it took Cain. Genesis 4:8 says, "Cain attacked his brother Abel and killed him." This happened despite the fact God warned Cain about the consequence of his anger and gave him an opportunity to turn things around.

It certainly appears Cain valued his anger and pride more than his relationship with his brother. God had told Cain how he could correct his situation if he wanted to. All Cain had to do was to give God what He had asked Cain to give him in the first place—the firstfruits of his crop. God also told Cain if he didn't correct the situation, he would be giving place to the Devil. Remember what God said to Cain in Genesis 4:6: "Then the Lord said to Cain, 'Why are you angry? Why is your face downcast? If you do what is right, will you not be accepted? But if you do not do what is right, sin is crouching at your door; it desires to have you, but you must master it.'"

It seems clear Cain was actually angry at God, but instead of directing his anger at God, he took it out on his brother Abel. Proverbs 29:22 says, "An angry man stirs up dissension, but a hot-tempered one commits many sins." Aristotle is credited with saying that anyone can become angry; that's easy. But to be angry with the right person, to the right degree, at the right time, for the right purpose and in the right way, that is not easy. I believe these words are right. It is so easy to take our anger out on whoever happens to be in our way.

Think about it. How many times have you gotten angry with someone at work and then gone home and taken it out on your family or friends? Or gotten angry at home and then taken it out on someone on the road or in the workplace?

Ecclesiastes 7:9 tells us, "Do not be quickly provoked in your spirit, for anger resides in the lap of fools." Proverbs 14:17 says, "A quick tempered man does foolish things."

When anger begins to rule your life, it will come out on anyone in any place at any time. You will even take your anger out on people who love and care about you. Eventually, the people you are directing your anger toward will not want to be around you. Often they don't know how to respond to you because some days you're happy and some days you're mad or upset. They may even become afraid to talk to you, since they know if they say something you don't like, you will get angry and lose control. Sooner or later, those who live in the house with an angry person will become angry themselves and end up living a miserable life as well.

My daddy was a hard and angry man who liked to take his rage out on others. It didn't take much to get him upset and, once he was, he just reacted and went to the extreme. He was always striking out. There were so many times when my daddy would get into a fight with my mother. I remember seeing my daddy hit my mother, as they called each other names and cursed at each other. I also remember my daddy beating my brothers and sisters, but especially me. He'd whip me with whatever he could get his hands on. Hose pipes, extensions cords, fan belts——he didn't care what he used. When he got angry, he was totally out of control.

I will never forget the day my daddy jumped on me about something I had stolen from him. He reached out and pushed me, demanding I give back the things I'd taken. My daddy had been shoving me around all of my life, but I'd had enough. I was fourteen years old and finally big enough to stand up to him. I wasn't going to let him beat me any more, so I pushed my father back as hard as I could. He stumbled backwards, but recovered in time to grab a hammer out of a nearby chair. He was shaking all over, and he only shook like that when he got really, really angry. I knew I was in for trouble. Sure enough, he raised the hammer over his head, shouting at me that he was going to knock my brains out. In response, I found myself shouting right back at my daddy saying that if he did, I was going to kill him.

My threats didn't stop my daddy. He pushed me again, and when he did, I reached up under my shirt, pulled out the gun I had in the waist of my pants and took a shot at him. My anger was so out of control it had brought me to the point of trying to kill my own father. Thank the Lord I missed him completely. The bullet flew past him and left a little hole in the screen porch that's still there today—a little reminder to me of just how far anger will take you.

You may be asking yourself how I sank to the place I would I try to kill my own father. The answer is simply this—if you don't deal with your anger, sooner or later, it will destroy your relationships with people, even those you're supposed to love.

MAKING IT PERSONAL

What about you? How are your relationships? Are they suffering because of your anger? What will it take for you to realize your anger is hurting those around you? THINKING IT OVER

- Do you feel like your relationships with family members, co-workers, or fellow students are going badly because of your anger?

- Have others talked to you about your anger and your attitude? If so, did you respond by listening or by striking out?
- Do you think it is possible people let you have your way because they are afraid of you or your reactions?
- Which is more important to you, your family and friends or your anger and negative attitude?

TAKING A POSITIVE ACTION STEP

- Identify someone you think may be afraid of you because of your anger. It might be your spouse, your parents, your siblings, or even one of your own children. It could also be a friend, co-worker, or simply an acquaintance. Whoever it is, find an opportunity to ask them if they are afraid of you. If the answer is yes, be prepared to apologize to them. Then consider following that up by asking God to set both of you free from your anger.
- Think of somebody you used to be in relationship with but drove off as a result of your anger. If it is appropriate, look them up. Admit your past attitude and then try to re-establish a kind and loving relationship with them.

TALKING TO GOD

Lord God, forgive me for all the people I've driven away because of my anger. I'm truly sorry for the pain I've caused them. Show me how not to let anger cause me to do or say things to hurt other people. Enable me by Your power to walk in love and to appreciate others more than my anger. In Jesus' name. AMEN.

HEARING GOD'S WORD

Fathers, do not exasperate your children; instead, bring them up in the training and instruction of the Lord.

—Ephesians 6:4

Wives, submit to your husbands, as is fitting in the Lord.

Husbands, love your wives and do not be harsh with them.

Children, obey your parents in everything, for this pleases the Lord.

Fathers, do not embitter your children, or they will become discouraged.

—Colossians 3:18-21

He who sows wickedness reaps trouble, and the rod of his fury will be destroyed.

—Proverbs 22:8

An angry man stirs up dissension, and a hot-tempered one commits many sins.

—Proverbs 29:22

Do not be quickly provoked in your spirit, for anger resides in the lap of fools.

—Ecclesiastes 7:9

A quick tempered man does foolish things, and a crafty man is hated.

—Proverbs 14:17

Seven

Anger Desensitizes
Your Heart

Then the Lord said to Cain, "Where is your brother Abel?" "I don't know," he replied. "Am I my brother's keeper?"

—Genesis 4:9

Scripture tells us that when God asked Cain where his brother Abel was, Cain responded to God this way: "'I don't know,' he replied. 'Am I my brother's keeper?'"

Can you imagine how callous and hardhearted you'd have to be to respond to God's question like that? This response is even more startling in light of the fact that Cain knew he'd just killed Abel. Cain's heart, however, was filled with such hatred and bitterness he could not show any remorse or concern over what he'd just done.

If you find Cain's behavior surprising, consider for a minute how you respond when you've hurt or harmed your father, mother, husband, wife, son, or daughter? Do you feel sorry? Or like Cain do you also have no remorse? Think back to the last time you hurt someone. How did you feel? Perhaps you didn't feel anything or maybe you felt a little sorry, but you sure weren't going to let it show. If either of these was your response, I want to warn you that you are walking on dangerous ground.

When you are not sensitive to the pain you're causing others, you'll find yourself going to the extreme. Eventually you will lose sight of how bad you're hurting that loved one, friend, or co-worker, and you will allow your anger to cause you to have the same attitude as Cain, desensitizing your heart and mind. Once you've grown callous, hardhearted, and uncaring about others, it becomes just all about how you feel.

I look back and remember a time when it was clear how insensitive my heart had become. It took place one afternoon in 1979 when I went into a house in Greenville to steal. I pushed a gun down into a sleeping man's face demanding money. When I did, he woke up out of a dead sleep begging me not to kill him. Even though I could hear his cries, my anger had desensitized my heart so much I could not respond to that cry. The only thing I could hear was my own anger and my rage. Instinctively, the man reached up and tried to grab the gun. As soon as he did, I began hitting him with the butt of the weapon. I could hear him crying out to me for mercy, but I just kept on hitting him. I couldn't find any stopping point, not even with him begging for his life. I kept on hitting the man until he lay there totally unconscious. His cries for help meant nothing to me. I simply took his money and left him for dead. You could say I had that Cain attitude.

MAKING IT PERSONAL

What about you? Are you so callous and hardhearted you can not hear the cries of those you've hurt in the past or those you're hurting now? You must remember that the more you give in to your anger, the more insensitive and callous you will become to others.

You might be saying in your heart right now that you can identify with what I'm saying, but you don't know how to change. Well, you've already done the first thing you need to do in order to change by recognizing you have a problem that needs to be addressed. 1 John 1:9 tells us, "If we confess our sins, he is faithful and just and will forgive our sins and purify us from all

ANGER DESENSITIZES YOUR HEART

unrighteousness." You might be asking if God will really forgive you for all the hurt and pain you've inflicted on others. The answer is yes. Think about David. He was a man who'd committed many sins including adultery and murder. David tells us in Psalms 32:5, "Then I acknowledged my sin to you and did not cover up my iniquity. I said, 'I will confess my transgressions to the Lord'—and you forgave the guilt of my sin."

If you want to change your hard heart, hear what Paul tells us in Romans 6:12-14:

> Therefore do not let sin reign in your moral body so that you obey its evil desires. Do not offer the parts of your body to sin, as instruments of wickedness, but rather offer yourselves to God, as those who have been brought from death to life, and offer the parts of your body to him as instruments of righteousness. For sin shall not be your master, because you are not under law, but under grace.

God can change you if you will allow him to or you can stay the same and keep on hurting others until you have completely destroyed them and yourself as well. What will it be? I hope you are thinking it over.

THINKING IT OVER

- Do you find it easy to hurt someone with your words or actions?
- Do you take pleasure in getting revenge?
- Are you afraid to show emotions and feelings because of your hurt and anger?
- How do you feel when you hurt or disappoint others?

TAKING A POSITIVE ACTION STEP

- Pick out someone you normally treat in a hostile or unkind way. The next time you see them, try treating them kindly. If you find it difficult to do this, ask God to make your heart tender toward others. When you get another opportunity, try

91

again to be loving and thoughtful toward that same person. If you fail again, don't give up. Ask God again to do what needs to be done to change your heart.

- Try to practice walking in the Spirit this week. If you are not a true believer, you will find it impossible to do, because before you can be led by the Holy Spirit, you must accept Jesus Christ as your Savior. If you are a true believer, you have the ability to walk in the Spirit, but may be unable to because you are walking in the flesh instead. If this is the case, you need to confess the situation to the Lord and ask him to enable you to walk in the Spirit instead of in the flesh.

TALKING TO GOD

Enable me, Lord, to let go of the past so I will not allow past hurts to harden my heart. Teach me how to love and how not to be ashamed to express that love to others. Soften my heart so I can be tender and kindhearted toward those around me. I ask this in the name of Jesus. Amen.

HEARING GOD'S WORD

The Lord said to Cain, "Where is your brother Abel?" "I don't know," he replied. "Am I my brother's keeper?"

—Genesis 4:9

Refrain from anger and turn from wrath; do not fret—it leads only to evil.

—Psalm 37:8

If we confess our sins, he is faithful and just and will forgive us our sins and purify us from all unrighteousness.

—1 John 1:9

Then I acknowledged my sin to you and did not cover up my iniquity. I said, "I will confess my transgressions to the Lord"—and you forgave the guilt of my sin.

—Psalm 32:5

But the fruit of the Spirit is love, joy, peace, patience, kindness, goodness, faithfulness, gentleness, and self-control. Against such things there is no law. Those who belong to Christ Jesus have crucified the sinful nature with its passions and desires. Since we live by the Spirit, let us keep in step with the Spirit.

—Galatians 5:22-26

Therefore do not let sin reign in your mortal body so that you obey its evil desires. Do not offer the parts of your body to sin, as instruments of wickedness, but rather offer yourselves to God, as those who have been brought from death to life, and offer the parts of your body to him as instruments of righteousness.

—Romans 6:12-13

Eight

Anger Will Cost You More Than You Want to Pay

Cain said to the Lord, "My punishment is more than I can bear."
—Genesis 4:13

Not only does anger desensitize your heart to the hurt you're doing to others, it also blinds you to the consequences of your actions. I believe Cain never thought he would end up in the predicament he found himself in once he failed to deal with his anger.

You remember God had warned Cain if he did not do something about his anger, the opportunity to do something foolish lay at the door of his heart, but Cain did not heed the warning God gave him. God is giving you and me that same warning. Fill in your name in the section of Scripture from Genesis 4 where God spoke to Cain:

Then the Lord said to_____, "Why are you angry? Why is your face downcast? If you, _____, do what is right, will you not be accepted? But if you, _____, do not do what is right, sin is crouching at your door; it desires to have _____, but you must master it."

Don't be like Cain and ignore the warning signs you are receiving right now about your anger. Paul tells us in Ephesians 4:30-32, "And do not grieve the Holy Spirit of God, with whom you were sealed for the day of redemption. Get rid of all bitterness, rage and anger, brawling and slander, along with every form of malice. Be kind and compassionate to one another, forgiving each other, just as in Christ God forgave you."

Once Cain ignored God's warning and let his anger drive him to sin by killing his brother, God told Cain what the consequences of his choice would be. Genesis 4:12 tells us what those were:

"The Lord said, 'What have you done? Listen! Your brother's blood cried out to me from the ground. Now you are under a curse and driven from the ground, which opened its mouth to receive your brother's blood from your hand. When you work the ground, it will no longer yield its crops for you. You will be a restless wanderer on the earth.'"

Now, listen to Cain's response to God's words: "'My punishment is more than I can bear.'"

Cain was saying his anger had cost him more than he wanted to pay. Proverbs 22:8 says, "He who sows iniquity will reap sorrow." Paul tells us in Galatians 6:7 "Do not be deceived: God cannot be mocked. A man reaps what he sows."

I remember reading once in the newspaper about a case of road rage which took place in the state of Alabama. The article reported that two women on the interstate in separate cars braked to avoid a truck pulling out from the roadside and nearly hit each other. When this happened, one of the women got mad at the other one and rammed her car into the other woman's vehicle. Both cars overturned and the woman who'd started the confrontation was ejected from her vehicle along with two infants in the car with her. The two babies who were thrown from the car suffered head trauma and had to be flown to the hospital; one later died. The tragedy of the whole case is that because of her uncontrolled anger, the mother had caused the death of her own child and she will have to live with that reality for the rest of her life.

When I was growing up, I too hurt many people, even my own family members, because of my anger. Yet, I was so blinded to the consequences of my actions I couldn't see how my anger was leading me down a road of destruction. My eyes were finally opened the day I found myself standing before a judge charged with armed robbery and attempted murder. I'd almost taken a man's life, despite the fact that he was begging me not to hurt him. Looking back I can see I was so intoxicated with anger I could not hear the man; all I could hear was my anger. So I kept on hitting him until he was unconscious. I actually thought I had probably killed the man. You might be asking how I could let myself get to this place. The answer is that I refused to deal with my anger until it got completely out of control.

As I stood in the courtroom before the judge, I knew I was facing death row if the man died. At last, I could hear all the people along the road who'd told me, "Eddie, you need to deal with your anger before you find yourself in a predicament you can't get out of and that will destroy you, your family, and your future." Only it was too late; I'd already reached that point. Thank God the man I'd beaten didn't die, so I only got ten years mandatory at Parchman Penitentiary and not the death penalty. As it turned out, my anger did not cost me my life, but it surely cost me more than I wanted to pay.

MAKING IT PERSONAL

What about you? What will have to happen in your life before you will realize you need to deal with your anger? Please don't allow something tragic to take place before you seek help. Remember sooner or later anger will always cost you more than you want to pay.

THINKING IT OVER

- Are there things you have already lost because of your anger? If so what?

- Is your bad temper keeping you from moving forward in life?
- Do anger and pride mean more to you than your family, your friends, and your future?
- What will it take for you to realize your anger is costing you more than you are able to pay or replace?

TAKING A POSITIVE ACTION STEP

- Make a list of all the opportunities and relationships anger has cost you. Ask God to show you everything that should be on the list. Put a check by each one of these you would like to get back. Ask God to reveal to you what it would take to make that possible.
- Try to drop your pride for just one day. If you can't, it is likely your anger is damaging you, your family, or your future, and you must deal with it right now before it is too late.

TALKING TO GOD

Lord God, give me wisdom to know how not to let my anger destroy me, my family, and my future. Keep me from being blind to the damage and pain my anger is costing me and others around me. Show me all this before it is too late. I ask this in Jesus' name. AMEN.

HEARING FROM GOD'S WORD

Cain said to the Lord, "My punishment is more than I can bear."
—Genesis 4:13

There is a way that seems right to a man, but in the end it leads to death.
—Proverbs 14:12-13

Then the Lord said to Cain, "Why are you angry? Why is your face downcast? If you do what is right, will you not be accepted? But if you do not do what is right, sin is crouching at your door; it desires to have you, but you must master it."

—Genesis 4:6-8

And do not grieve the Holy Spirit of God, with whom you were sealed for the day of redemption. Get rid of all bitterness, rage, and anger, brawling and slander, along with every form of malice. Be kind and compassionate to one another, forgiving each other, just as in Christ God forgave you.

—Ephesians 4:30-32

He who sows wickedness reaps trouble, and the rod of his fury will be destroyed.

—Proverbs 22:8

Do not be deceived: God cannot be mocked. A man reaps what he sows. The one who sows to please his sinful nature, from that nature will reap destruction; the one who sows to please the Spirit, from the Spirit will reap eternal life.

—Galatians 6:7-8

Part III
Seven Steps to Putting Out the Fire of Your Anger

Now that you've seen the negative effects uncontrolled anger can have on your life, perhaps you are ready to take the steps you need to take in order to put out the fire of your anger. If you don't, anger will eventually cost you more than you want to pay. Don't wait until then. Now is the time to do something about your situation. Let's learn how.

Ask Jesus Christ into Your Life

"The word is near you; it is in your mouth and in your heart," that is, the word of faith we are proclaiming: That if you confess with your mouth, "Jesus Christ is Lord," and believe in your heart that God raised him from the dead, you will be saved. For it is with your heart that you believe and are justified, and it is with your mouth that you confess and are saved.

—Romans 10:8-10

The only truly effective way for you to change your life and deal with your anger is by allowing God to do that for you. Self-discipline and self-help can go just so far. God alone can bring about the deep heart change needed to truly set you free from bondage to self and sin. In order for this to be possible, you must first come into relationship with God by asking Jesus Christ into your heart.

If you have never entered into a real relationship with the Lord Jesus Christ, you can do that right now or anytime you feel ready to do this. God is waiting for you to take that step. When you make the decision to ask the Lord Jesus Christ into your life, Jesus will come in and forgive you of all your sin.

If you would, read Romans 10:8-10 again. Notice it says if you believe in your heart God loves you so much that He sent His son,

Jesus Christ, to die for you, you can be saved and live a new life. The Bible tells us in John 3:16, "For God so loved the world that he gave his one and only Son, that whoever believes in him shall not perish but have eternal life." What a gift God has given you and me, but we must accept that gift before we can have a personal relationship with Him and receive the promise of a new life.

You might be asking yourself, "Can God really love a person like me? My life is really messed up and my attitude is so bad it has destroyed many things. Can God forgive me of all the wrongs I've done? Would God really want to change me?"

The answer is yes. Absolutely yes. Listen to what God says in Isaiah 1:18:"'Come now, let us reason together,' says the Lord. 'Though your sins are like scarlet, they shall be as white as snow; though they are red as crimson, they shall be like wool.'"

God is not waiting until you get yourself together to love you and come into your life. Instead, he loves you right now just as you are and wants to be a part of your life starting today. My own life is a testimony to this. The night I accepted Jesus Christ as my Lord and Savior, I was actually sitting on my cot in Parchman Penitentiary contemplating murdering two men just to increase my prison reputation as a tough guy. Yet, despite that, God out of his grace and love heard my cry for help and turned my life around.

The Bible tells us in Romans 5:6, 8 "You see, at just the right time, when we were still powerless, Christ died for the ungodly. But God demonstrates his own love for us in this: While we were still sinners, Christ died for us."

Can you see how much God loves you? Are you ready to accept that love?

As the Scripture says, 'Anyone who trusts in him will never be put to shame.'" The question is will you let Jesus in?

It doesn't matter how messed up your life is or how bad your temper is, God can change things. Isaiah 55:6-7 also says, "Seek the Lord while He may be found, call upon Him while he is near. Let the wicked forsake his way, and the unrighteous man his thoughts. Let him return to the Lord, and He will have mercy on him, and to our God, for He will abundantly pardon."

The Lord Jesus Christ guarantees you He can change your life and attitude by making you a new person. 2 Corinthians 5:17 puts that promise this way: "Therefore, if anyone is in Christ, he is a new creation; old things have passed away; behold all things have become new."

You might be asking this question: When can I begin to experience this newness of life? The answer is right now. Once you have let the Lord Jesus Christ into your life, the process can start right that very minute. 1 John 1:9-10 says, "If we confess our sins, he is faithful and just to forgive us our sins and to cleanse us from all unrighteousness."

The decision is yours. What will you do? Remember your anger will surely change your life, but in ways that could cost you everything. Which will it be? Will you continue to live life your way or will you begin to live it God's Way?

TALKING TO GOD

If you are ready to choose God's Way, then pray this prayer:

Father God, Your Word says if I confess with my mouth that Jesus is Lord and believe in my heart that You have raised Jesus from the dead, I will be saved. Therefore, Father, I confess that Jesus is Lord. I believe in my heart that You, Father God, raised Jesus from the dead. I ask You, Lord Jesus, to come into my heart right now. I renounce my past life and my anger. Forgive me for sinning against You. I believe You are now my Lord and Savior, and I have become a new creation by the power of the Holy Spirit. AMEN

If you are considering it but not yet ready to give God control over your life, pray this prayer:

Father God, I see in Your Word that You love me and have made provision for my sin and my anger through Your Son, Jesus Christ. Right now, though, I'm not ready to accept Your gift of salvation. Change my heart according to Your will so that I will come to the place I'm ready to do that. In Christ's name. AMEN

If you believe that you have accepted Christ as your Savior in the past, but are not living as a new creation, pray this prayer:

Lord Jesus, I confess I've sinned against You by turning my back on the salvation You've provided me through Your son, Jesus Christ. Thank You for remaining faithful during my unfaithfulness and for not turning Your back on me. I want You to take control of my life again and enable me to overcome my anger. I ask You by Your grace and mercy to forgive me of all my sins and do what only You can do in my life. In Christ's name. AMEN

HEARING GOD'S WORD

If we confess our sins, he is faithful and just and will forgive us our sins and purify us from all unrighteousness.
—1 John 1:8-10

For God so loved the world that he gave his one and only Son, that whoever believes in him shall not perish but have eternal life.
—John 3:16

Yet to all who received him, to those who believed in his name, he gave the right to become children of God.
—John 1:12

But God demonstrates his own love for us in this: While we were still sinners, Christ died for us.
—Romans 5:8

For the wages of sin is death, but the gift of God is eternal life in Christ Jesus our Lord.
—Romans 6:23

Therefore, if anyone is in Christ, he is a new creation; the old has gone, the new has come!
—2 Corinthians 5:17

"The word is near you; it is in your mouth and in your heart," that is, the word of faith we are proclaiming: That if you confess with your

mouth, "Jesus is Lord," and believe in your heart that God raised
him from the dead, you will be saved. For it is with your heart that
you believe and are justified, and it is with your mouth that you
confess and are saved.

—Romans 10:8-10

"Come now, let us reason together," says the Lord. "Though your
sins are like scarlet, they shall be as white as snow; though they are
red as crimson, they shall be like wool."

—Isaiah 1:18

Seek the Lord while he may be found; call on him while he is near.
Let the wicked forsake his way and the evil man his thoughts. Let
him turn to the Lord, and he will have mercy on him, and to our
God, for he will freely pardon.

—Isaiah 55:6-7

Step Two

Submit to the Leading and Power of the Holy Spirit

So I say, live by the Spirit, and you will not gratify the desires of the sinful nature. For the sinful nature desires what is contrary to the Spirit, and the Spirit what is contrary to the sinful nature. They are in conflict with each other, so that you do not do what you want.
—Galatians 5:16-17

O nce you are saved, you must allow the Holy Spirit to lead you so you can become the person God wants you to be. He doesn't want you to be the angry, resentful, bitter, or quick-tempered person you've been for so long; God wants you to be the new person you are in Christ. You no longer have to stay that old person who couldn't help reacting to everything. Paul says in 2 Corinthians 5:17, "Therefore if anyone (that means you!) is in Christ, he is a new creation; the old has gone, the new has come."

As a believer, God has given you the Holy Spirit to help you mature in your relationship with Him. Galatians 5:16, Amplified, puts it this way: "But I say, walk and live habitually in the (Holy) Spirit—responsive to, and controlled and guided by the Spirit; then you will certainly not gratify the cravings and desires of the flesh—of human nature without God." This simply means you are to walk one step at a time controlled by the Spirit of God, no longer a slave to your own sinful urges and desires.

The more you let the power of the Holy Spirit work in your life, the stronger you will get. Paul tells us whatever we give ourselves to will have dominion over our lives. If we give ourselves to anger, anger will control our lives. If we give ourselves to the Holy Spirit, He will control our lives. When we do this, the result is what is described in Romans 6:11:"In the same way, count yourselves dead to sin (in this case, anger), but alive to God in Christ Jesus. Therefore do not let sin (anger) reign in your mortal body so that you obey its evil desires."

Once you are in Christ, you no longer have to let your anger get out of control every time someone or something upsets you. Ephesians 4:26-27 says, "'In your anger do not sin': Do not let the sun go down while you are still angry and do not give a foothold to the devil." When Paul tells us not to give a foothold to the Devil, he means don't give the Devil an opportunity to control or influence your life.

You might be asking the question right now, "If I do get mad and lose control of my temper does that mean I'm not saved?" No, it doesn't. You are saved if you have sincerely asked the Lord Jesus Christ to come into your life. Keep in mind that even though salvation is certain and lasts forever, spiritual victory is a day by day, moment by moment experience of depending on the Holy Spirit. If you give in to the flesh by becoming angry or sinning, you will lose every time. On the other hand, if you let the Holy Spirit control you, you will have victory. If not, you will continue to give anger or other sin a place in your life. You must make the choice. Listen to the question Paul asked in Romans 6:16-18, "Don't you know that when you offer yourselves to someone to obey him as slaves, you are slaves to the one whom you obey—whether you are slaves to sin which leads to death, or of obedience which leads to righteousness? But thanks be to God that, though you used to be slaves to sin, you wholeheartedly obeyed the form of teaching to which you were entrusted. You have been set free from sin and have becomes slaves to righteousness."

When I first got saved, I thought it was impossible for me to change. I still felt like I had to give in to my anger. Then I read

Romans 8:12-14:"Therefore, brothers, we have an obligation—but it is not to the sinful nature, to live according to it. For if you live according to the sinful nature, you will die; but if by the Spirit you put to death the misdeeds of the body, you will live, because those who are led by the Spirit of God are sons of God. For you did not receive a spirit that makes you a slave again to fear, but you received the Spirit of sonship."

This Scripture told me that I wasn't obligated to give in to my anger because I was a new person in the Lord Jesus Christ. Once I actually understood that truth, the circumstances of my life began to change as I allowed God by the power of the Holy Spirit to do in my life what I couldn't do myself.

Guess what? You aren't obligated to continue in sin and anger either! If you are saved, you are a new person in Christ. You're not the same; you can become a changed person. It might help to remind yourself often of the truth of 2 Corinthians 5:17:"Therefore, if anyone is in Christ, he is a new creation; the old has gone, the new has come!"

TALKING TO GOD

Father God, thank You for the Holy Spirit You've sent to lead me in the way You want me to go and to teach me the things You want me to know. I realize that without Your Holy Spirit leading me, my life will be out of control. I ask your forgiveness for trying to do my own thing and to have my own way. Strengthen me with the mighty power of the Holy Spirit. Teach me to walk in love, not in anger. Empower me to let go of the things that upset me and not allow them to rule over my life. I ask this in the name of Jesus. AMEN.

HEARING GOD'S WORD

Therefore, since we are surrounded by such a great cloud of witnesses, let us throw off everything that hinders and the sin that so easily entangles, and let us run with perseverance the race marked out for us.

—Hebrews 12:1-2

But now you must rid yourselves of all such things as these: anger, rage, malice, slander, and filthy language from your lips.

—*Colossians 3:8*

You were taught, with regard to your former way of life, to put off your old self, which is being corrupted by its deceitful desires; to be made new in the attitude of your minds; and to put on the new self, created to be like God in true righteousness and holiness.

—*Ephesians 4:22-24*

So I say, live by the Spirit, and you will not gratify the desires of the sinful nature. For the sinful nature desires what is contrary to the Spirit, and the Spirit what is contrary to the sinful nature.

—*Galatians 5:16-17*

In the same way, count yourselves dead to sin but alive to God in Christ Jesus. Therefore do not let sin reign in your mortal body so that you obey its evil desires. Do not offer the parts of your body to sin, as instruments of wickedness, but rather offer yourselves to God, as those who have been brought from death to life; and offer the parts of your body to him as instruments of righteousness. For sin shall not be your master, because you are not under law, but under grace.

What then? Shall we sin because we are not under law but under grace? By no means! Don't you know that when you offer yourselves to someone to obey him as slaves, you are slaves to the one whom you obey—whether you are slaves to sin, which leads to death, or to obedience, which leads to righteousness?

—*Romans 6:11-16*

Those who live according to the sinful nature have their minds set on what that nature desires; but those who live in accordance with the Spirit have their minds set on what the Spirit desires. The mind of sinful man is death, but the mind controlled by the Spirit is life and peace; the sinful mind is hostile to God. It does not submit to God's law, nor can it do so. Those controlled by the sinful nature cannot please God.

You, however, are controlled not by the sinful nature but by the Spirit, if the Spirit of God lives in you. And if anyone does not have the Spirit of Christ, he does not belong to Christ. But if Christ is in you, your body is dead because of sin, yet your spirit is alive because of righteousness. And if the Spirit of him who raised Jesus from the dead is living in you, he who raised Christ from the dead will also give life to your mortal bodies through his Spirit, who lives in you.

—Romans 8:5-11

In the same way, the Spirit helps us in our weakness. We do not know what we ought to pray for, but the Spirit himself intercedes for us with groans that words cannot express. And he who searches our hearts knows the mind of the Spirit, because the Spirit intercedes for the saints according to God's will.

And we know that in all things God works for the good of those who love him, who have been called according to his purpose.

—Romans 8:26-28

Step Three

Spend Time in the Word of God on a Regular Basis

I have hidden your word in my heart that I might not sin against you.

—Psalm 119:11

In order to get control of your anger, it is important for you to grow strong in your relationship with the Lord. To do that, it is essential for you to spend time in the Word of God. Just like physical growth depends on what a person eats, spiritual growth depends on "feeding on" or studying the Word of God.

David tells us in Psalm 1:1-4, "Blessed is the man (that is you!) who does not walk in the counsel of the wicked or stand in the way of sinners or sit in the seat of mockers. But his delight is in the law (Word) of the Lord, and on his law he mediates (studies or eats) day and night. He is like a tree planted by streams of water, which yields its fruit in season and whose leaf does not wither. Whatever he does prospers. Not so the wicked! They are like chaff that the wind blows away."

The more you feed on the Word of God, the stronger you will become in your spiritual life. It is also true that the less you feed your anger, the weaker it will become. Whatever you feed the most will be stronger. Dr. Billy Graham likes to tell the story about an

Eskimo fisherman who came to town every Saturday afternoon bringing his two dogs with him. One was white; the other was black. He had taught them to fight on command. Every Saturday afternoon in the town square people would gather and these two dogs would fight while the fisherman took bets. One Saturday the black dog would win; another Saturday, the white dog would win—but the fisherman always won. When his friends began to ask him how he did it, the fisherman replied, "I starve one and feed the other. The one I feed always wins, because he is stronger."

There will be many occasions when your anger will be begging you to feed it, but keep in mind that the less you feed it, the weaker it will become.

Paul admonished young Timothy—and also you and me—about how important the Word of God is to us. 2 Timothy 3:14-17 says, "But as for you, continue in what you have learned and have become convinced of, because you know those from whom you learned it, and how from infancy you have known the holy Scriptures, which are able to make you wise for salvation through faith in Christ Jesus. All Scripture is God-breathed and is useful for teaching, rebuking, correcting and training in righteousness, so that the man of God may be thoroughly equipped for every good work."

David says in Psalms 119:9-11. "How can a young man keep his way pure? By living according to your word. I seek you with all my heart; do not let me stray from your commands. I have hidden your word in my heart that I might not sin against you."

Psalm 119:105 goes on to say, "Your word is a lamp to my feet and a light for my path." And Psalm 119:133 says, "Direct my footsteps according to your word; let no sin rule over me."

And Hebrews 4:12 says: "For the word of God is living and active. Sharper than any double-edge sword, it penetrates even to dividing soul and spirit, joints and marrow; it judges the thought and attitudes of the heart."

Let me remind you again that the less you feed your anger, the weaker it will become, and the more you feed on the Word of God, the stronger your faith will grow. Any day allowed to pass without reading God's Word is a day in which your heart and life are open to sin and anger.

D.L. Moody once said, "In prayer we talk to God. In Bible study, God talks to us, and we had better let God do most of the talking."

Make it a regular daily habit to let God speak to you as you read your Bible. It may take time to cultivate this as a regular part of your day, but, if you want to grow as a believer and get control of your anger, it is essential.

TALKING TO GOD

Father, teach me to mediate on Your Word every day so I will learn more about You and Your ways. Transform my life with Your Word and renew my mind so I will be able to get control of my anger. I ask this in the name of Jesus. AMEN.

HEARING GOD'S WORD

For the word of God is living and active. Sharper than any double-edged sword, it penetrates even to dividing soul and spirit, joints and marrow; it judges the thoughts and attitudes of the heart.
—Hebrews 4:12

Do your best to present yourself to God as one approved, a work-man who does not need to be ashamed and who correctly handles the word of truth.
—I Timothy 2:15

How can a young man keep his way pure? By living according to your word.

I seek you with all my heart; do not let me stray from your commands. I have hidden your word in my heart that I might not sin against you.
—Psalm 119:9-11

Your word is a lamp to my feet and a light for my path.
—Psalm 119:105

Direct my footsteps according to your word; let no sin rule over me.

—Psalm 119:133

Blessed is the man who does not walk in the counsel of the wicked or stand in the way of sinners or sit in the seat of mockers. But his delight is in the law (Word) of the Lord and on his law (Word) he meditates day and night. He is like a tree planted by streams of water which yields its fruit in season and whose leaf does not wither. Whatever he does prospers. Not so the wicked! They are like chaff that the wind blows away."

—Psalm 1:1-4

Step Four
Talk to God in Prayer

The Lord is near to all who call on him, to all who call on him in truth.

—Psalm 145:18

E. M. Bounds once said, "In dealing with mankind, nothing is more important to God than prayer. Prayer is likewise of great importance to people. Failure to pray is failure in all of life. It is failure of duty, service, and spiritual progress. It is only by prayer that God can help people."

In light of this truth, it is essential you learn to pray in order to strengthen your walk with the Lord and begin to overcome your past life.

You might be saying, "I am not good at praying!" or "I don't know how to pray!" May I ask you a question? Do you know how to talk? If so, you know how to pray, because prayer is simply talking to God. It isn't about how well or how eloquently you speak; it's about how real you are in your heart when you talk to God. God is never impressed with how skillful you are with words; he is only impressed when you pray from a real heart.

Our Lord Jesus Christ gave us a good example in Luke 18:10-14 of what it means to pray with a real and sincere heart: "Two men went up to the temple to pray, one a Pharisee and the other a tax collector. The Pharisee stood up and prayed about himself: 'God, I thank you that I am not like other men—robbers, evildoers, adulterers—or even like this tax collector. I fast twice a week and give a tenth of all I get.' But the tax collector stood at a distance. He would not even look up to heaven, but beat his breast and said, 'God, have mercy on me, a sinner.' I tell you that this man, rather than the other, went home justified before God. For everyone who exalts himself will be humbled, and he who humbles himself will be exalted."

When I first gave my life to the Lord Jesus Christ, I was afraid to pray, especially in front of others. Most of my fear came from the fact that I was uneducated and only read on the second grade level. In addition, at the time ninety-five percent of my vocabulary consisted of curse words. I was absolutely scared to death I might cuss or say the wrong thing. I didn't know God wasn't looking at how well I prayed, but at how sincere my heart was. The Bible says in Hebrews 11:6, "And without faith it is impossible to please God, because anyone who comes to him must believe that he exists and that he rewards those who earnestly seek him." James 4:2-3 says, "You do not have, because you do not ask God. When you ask, you do not receive, because you ask with wrong motives, that you may spend what you get on your pleasures."

You might be asking yourself, "Can I pray to God if I'm upset or angry about something or with someone?" The answer is yes, you can. In fact, God wants you to call on Him when you are facing difficult moments in your life. I want you to hear from Psalm 4:1 how David prayed when he was facing difficulties in his life: "Answer me when I call to you, O my righteous God. Give me relief from my distress; be merciful to me and hear my prayer." David also prayed in Psalm 25:1:"The troubles of my heart have multiplied; free me from my anguish." And in Psalm 77:1-4:"I cried out to God for help; I cried out to God to hear me. When I was in distress, I sought the Lord; at night I stretched out untiring hands and my soul refused to be comforted. I remembered you, O God, and I groaned; I mused and my spirit grew faint. You kept my eyes from closing; I was too troubled to speak." And finally from Psalm 118:5, "In my anguish I cried to the Lord, and he answered by setting me free."

God actually encourages us to call on Him when we are in trouble or upset or angry. Psalms 50:15 says: "Call upon me in the day of trouble; I will deliver you and you will honor me." Psalm 107:6 says, "Then they cried out to the Lord in their trouble, and he delivered them from their distress."

Allow the prayer that David prayed in Psalm 139:23-24 to be your prayer: "Search me, O God, and know my heart; test me and know my anxious thoughts. See if there is any offensive way in me, and lead me in the way everlasting." And, no matter what, make sure you begin to talk to God on a regular basis about what is going on in your life. You can start right now with the prayer that follows.

TALKING TO GOD

Father God, teach me to pray. Remove the fear from my heart, so I will not be afraid to come to You in prayer. Teach me how to listen to hear Your voice when I pray and give me the power to walk in obedience when You do speak to me. I am grateful for the privilege of coming to You and talking with You. In Jesus' name. AMEN

HEARING GOD'S WORD

Hear, O Lord, my righteous plea; listen to my cry. Give ear to my prayer—it does not rise from deceitful lips.
—Psalm 17:1

The Lord is near to all who call on him, to all who call on him in truth.
—Psalm 145:18

The Lord has heard my cry for mercy; the Lord accepts my prayer.
—Psalm 6:9

Listen to my prayer, O God, do not ignore my plea; hear me and answer me.

—*Psalm 55:1*

Evening, morning, and noon I cry out in distress, and he hears my voice.

—*Psalm 55:17*

"This, then, is how you should pray: 'Our Father in heaven, hallowed be your name, your kingdom come, your will be done on earth as it is in heaven. Give us this day our daily bread. Forgive us our debts, as we also have forgiven our debtors. And lead us not into temptation, but deliver us from the evil one.'"

—*Matthew 6:9-13*

"Ask and it will be given to you; seek and you will find; knock and the door will be opened to you. For everyone who asks receives; he who seeks finds; and to him who knocks, the door will be opened. Which of you, if his son asks for bread, will give him a stone? Or if he asks for a fish, will give him a snake? If you, then, though you are evil, know how to give good gifts to your children, how much more will your Father in heaven give good gifts to those who ask him! "

—*Matthew 7:7-11*

Pray continually.

—*1 Thessalonians 5:17*

Do not be anxious about anything, but in everything, by prayer and petition, with thanksgiving, present your requests to God. And the peace of God, which transcends all understanding, will guard your hearts and your minds in Christ Jesus.

—*Philippians 4:5-7*

Deal with Your Pride

God opposes the proud, but gives grace to the humble: Submit your-selves, then, to God. Resist the devil, and he will flee from you.
—James 4:6-7

As we've already seen, pride is one of the main contributing factors to anger. So many times it's not what others have done to you that upsets you; instead, it is your pride that will not allow you to let go of the things creating anger. For instance, if someone knocks you down or steps on your foot accidentally and you know it was unintentional, normally you will let it go. But, if your pride won't let you overlook it, you'll get mad instead and want to retaliate.

The Bible tells us in Proverbs 13:10, "Pride only breeds quarrels." If you want to overcome your anger, you must stop letting your pride cause you to make mountains out of mole hills.

If you look back over your life, you can probably see there were a lot of things you got angry about that should not have upset you, but your pride would not allow you to let it go and you ended up filled with anger. Or maybe you can recall times when you offended others, but your pride would not let you go and say you were sorry or ask for forgiveness. Simply because people are uneasy with words like "I was wrong" or 'Would you please forgive me?" or "I'm sorry" marriages are destroyed, families are broken apart, and friendships are lost. The sad thing is this often happens just because someone wants to keep their pride. Let me ask you what you are willing to sacrifice in order to hold on to your pride? Will it be your marriage, your family, a friendship, a job, or even your relationship with the Lord Jesus Christ?

You see, pride can keep you from surrendering your life to Christ because you don't want to confess you have a problem with anger. In order to get God's help, you must be willing to admit you can not control your temper and can not change your life. You must swallow your pride and admit you need help. Most importantly, you must humble yourself before the Lord and confess your shortcomings, admitting you can't overcome your anger without His help. You can keep your pride, but it will cost you everything. Is it worth that?

My question to you is: How long will you keep on letting your pride cause you to stay angry? Proverbs 16:18 says, "Pride goes before destruction, a haughty spirit before a fall." Furthermore, Paul tells us in Colossians 3:12-13, "Therefore, as God's chosen people, holy and dearly loved, clothe yourselves with compassion, kindness, humility, gentleness and patience. Bear with each other and forgive whatever grievances you may have against one another. Forgive as the Lord forgave you."

Paul also tells us in Ephesians 4:26-27, "'In your anger do not sin': Do not let the sun go down while you are still angry, and do not give the devil a foothold." In Ephesians 4:29-32, Paul says, "Do not let any unwholesome talk come out of your mouths, but only what is helpful for building others up according to their needs, that it may benefit those who listen. And do not grieve the Holy Spirit of God, with whom you were sealed for the day of redemption. Get rid of all bitterness, rage and anger, brawling and slander, along with every form of malice. Be kind and compassionate to one another, forgiving each other, just as in Christ God forgave you."

These Scriptures tell us in order to deal with pride we must be experiencing God's love and forgiveness. Once you are in relationship with Jesus Christ you have access to the power that will allow you to put aside your pride and begin to trust God with the circumstances of your life.

TALKING TO GOD

Father, You have told us that You resist the proud, but give grace to the humble. Forgive me, Father God, for allowing pride to control my life. I ask You to give me a spirit of humility and enable me to turn from my pride and experience Your grace. In Jesus' name. AMEN.

HEARING GOD'S WORD

Pride only breeds quarrels, but wisdom is found in those who take advice.
—Proverbs 13:10

Pride goes before destruction, a haughty spirit before a fall.
—Proverbs 16:18

"God opposes the proud but gives grace to the humble." Submit your-selves, then, to God. Resist the devil, and he will flee from you.
—James 4:6-7

For if you forgive men when they sin against you, your heavenly Father will also forgive you. But if you do not forgive men their sins, your Father will not forgive your sins.
—Matthew 6:14

Be kind and compassionate to one another, forgiving each other, just as in Christ God forgave you.
—Ephesians 4:32

Bear with each other and forgive whatever grievance you may have against one another. Forgive as the Lord forgave you.
—Colossians 3:13

Learn to Let Go of Things That Upset You

Therefore, since we are surrounded by such a great cloud of witnesses, let us throw off everything that hinders and the sin that so easily entangles, and let us run with perseverance the race marked out for us.

—*Hebrews 12:1*

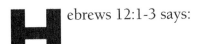ebrews 12:1-3 says:

Therefore, since we are surrounded by such a great cloud of witnesses, let us throw off everything that hinders and the sin that so easily entangles, and let us run with perseverance the race marked out for us. Let us fix our eyes on Jesus, the author and perfecter of our faith, who for the joy set before him endured the cross, scorning its shame, and sat down at the right hand of the throne of God. Consider him who endured such opposition from sinful men, so that you will not grow weary and lose heart.

I love these words and really believe you can find in them the confidence to put aside the things that upset you.

Perhaps you like your anger and think you want to hold on to it. After all, it seems to work. It gets you your way; it seems to give you power and control; and besides, you are very familiar and comfortable with the lifestyle of anger. But, remember eventually it will cost you more than you want to pay. So, now is the time to do something about putting out the fire of your anger.

It might be hard for you to let go of the things that upset you, but you must keep in mind that everything good will be a challenge—a challenge I believe you can win with the help of the Lord Jesus Christ. You must let him have those things that normally set you off if you want to get free from your anger. If you hold onto them, they will eventually destroy you, your family, and your future. The choice is yours.

Paul encourages us in Ephesians 4:22-24 when he says, "You were taught, with regard to your former way of life, to put off your old self, which is being corrupted by deceitful desires; to be made new in the attitude of your minds; and to put on the new self, created to be like God in true righteousness and holiness." Paul also tells us in Colossians 3:8, "But now you must rid yourselves of all such things as these: anger, rage, malice, slander, and filthy language from your lips."

You might be living by the same destructive motto I lived by, "An eye for an eye and a tooth for a tooth." Because it was hard for me to let go of things when someone made me angry, I would bottle up all my anger inside me. I felt like I had to get even. Eventually, my desire to hold onto my anger and to get even began to destroy my life and my relationship with others. I didn't realize at the time but my anger was just like a cancer eating me up on the inside. After I got saved, I prayed that the Lord would help me to let go of my anger and take away my desire to get even. With time, this became a reality in my life.

Paul tells us in Romans 12:17, 21, "Do not repay anyone evil for evil" and "Do not overcome by evil, but overcome evil with good." Paul also tells us in Ephesians 4:31-32, "Get rid of all bitterness, rage, and brawling and slander, along with every form of malice. Be kind and compassionate to one another, forgiving one another, just as in Christ God forgave you."

Perhaps these questions might be running though your mind right now: How can I let go of my anger when someone has made me mad? How can I give up the desire to seek revenge on the person who did me wrong? These are good and legitimate questions that demand answers. Letting go of your anger and hurt in your own ability is very hard. That's the reason the Bible lets us know that when we are in the Lord Jesus Christ He gives us the power and the ability to deal with anger and to forgive those who hurt us. Philippians 4:13 puts it this way: "I can do everything through him (Christ) who gives me strength." And, I love what the Lord said to Paul and also to you and to me in 2 Corinthians 12:9: "But he said to me, 'My grace is sufficient for you, for my power is made perfect in weakness. Therefore I will boast all the more gladly about my weaknesses, so that Christ's power may rest on me.'"

I have had to learn that real forgiveness doesn't mean I don't feel the hurt; it doesn't mean I won't think about it from time to time; it doesn't mean I won't have a desire for revenge; it doesn't mean I have to become my offender's best buddy; it doesn't mean I must allow that person to hurt me again; it doesn't mean the pain will go away overnight after I have forgiven the person who hurt me or made me angry. It does mean I can forgive those who've hurt me by giving it to the Lord and asking him to give me the power to forgive them.

Romans 12:17-20 tells us, "Do not repay anyone evil for evil. Be careful to do what is right in the eyes of everybody. If it is possible, as far as it depends on you, live at peace with everyone. Do not take revenge, my friends, but leave room for God's wrath, for it is written, 'It is mine to avenge; I will repay,' says the Lord."

Matthew 6:14-15 also reminds us how important it is to forgive and let go: "'For if you forgive men when they sin against you, your heavenly Father will also forgive you. But if you do not forgive men their sins, your Father will not forgive your sins.'"

Don't be afraid to let things go and to forgive others. You will benefit more by letting go than you will by holding on to your anger, hurt, and resentment. Why don't you free yourself by giving up what is keeping you angry? Maybe the following prayer will help.

TALKING TO GOD

Heavenly Father, I ask You to strengthen me with the mighty power of the Holy Spirit. Please forgive me for allowing anger to rule over my life. I surrender my quick temper to You and I also give You all the past hurts others have inflicted on me. Teach me to walk in love, not in anger. Empower me to let go of the things that upset me. I ask this in the name of Jesus. AMEN.

HEARING GOD'S WORD

Therefore, since we are surrounded by such a great cloud of witnesses, let us throw off everything that hinders and the sin that so easily entangles, and let us run with perseverance the race marked out for us.

—Hebrews 12:1-2

But now you must rid yourselves of all such things as these: anger, rage, malice, slander, and filthy language from your lips.

—Colossians 3:8

You were taught, with regard to your former way of life, to put off your old self, which is being corrupted by its deceitful desires; to be made new in the attitude of your minds; and to put on the new self, created to be like God in true righteousness and holiness.

—Ephesians 4:22-24

Know Who You Are in Christ

You, dear children, are from God and have overcome them, because the one who is in you is greater than the one who is in the world.
—1 John 4:4

Knowing who you are in Christ will enable you to find the hope and strength to deal with your anger and not let it control you any more.

Paul reminds us in Philippians 4:13 of the power we have in Christ when he says, "I can do all things through him (Christ) who gives me strength." He also tells us in 1 John 4:4, "You, dear children, are from God and have overcome them, because the one who is in you is greater than the one who is in the world."

Let me share with you what happened one day when I had been saved about a year. I was still locked up in prison and another inmate called me an insulting name. When he did, I got so angry I wanted to destroy him. All my life, when I'd gotten angry, I just reacted. This day, however, the Holy Spirit reminded me I no longer had to do what my mind was telling me to do. These were the words I sensed in my heart: "Eddie, you are not who you used to be; you are changed. You can choose to let this go, or you can hold on to your anger." Surprisingly, I found myself letting it go.

Once I did, I felt so good knowing I was not the same old person, but a new person in Christ.

In 2 Corinthians 5:17, Paul tells us what happens in our lives when we become a believer: "Therefore, if anyone is in Christ, he is a new creation; the old has gone, the new has come."

Peter speaks to this same matter when he says in 1 Peter 1:18-19: "For you know that it was not with perishable things such as silver or gold that you were redeemed from the empty way of life handed down to you from your forefathers, but with the precious blood of Christ, a lamb without blemish or defect." Peter also encourages us to remember who we are in Christ in 1 Peters 2:9-11:

> But you are a chosen people, a royal priesthood, a holy nation, a people belonging to God, that you may declare the praises of him who called you out of darkness into his wonderful light. Once you were not a people, but now you are the people of God; once you had not received mercy, but now you have received mercy. Dear friends, I urge you, as aliens and strangers in the world, to abstain from sinful desires, which war against your soul.

Keep in mind exactly who you are in the Lord Jesus Christ and what He has done for you. If you will, it can help you overcome your anger no matter what comes your way. 2 Corinthians 2:14 might be a good Scripture to use: "But thanks be to God, who always leads us in triumphal procession in Christ and through us spreads everywhere the fragrance of the knowledge of him."

TALKING TO GOD

> Lord God, I thank You that I am Your workmanship created in Christ Jesus. I believe You have delivered me from the dominion of darkness and brought me into Your light. Thank You, Lord, for giving me the power to control my anger, to forgive, and to let things go as well as for making me a free person. In Jesus' name. AMEN.

HEARING GOD'S WORD

> But you are a chosen people, a royal priesthood, a holy nation, a people belonging to God, that you may declare the praises of him

who called you out of darkness into his wonderful light. Once you were not a people, but now you are the people of God; once you had not received mercy, but now you have received mercy.

—1 Peter 2:9-10

For you know that it was not with perishable things such as silver or gold that you were redeemed from the empty way of life handed down to you from your forefathers, but with the precious blood of Christ, a lamb without blemish or defect.

—1 Peter 1:18-19

For this reason, ever since I heard about your faith in the Lord Jesus and your love for all the saints, I have not stopped giving thanks for you, remembering you in my prayers. I keep asking that the God of our Lord Jesus Christ, the glorious Father, may give you the Spirit of wisdom and revelation, so that you may know him better. I pray also that the eyes of your heart may be enlightened in order that you may know the hope to which he has called you, the riches of his glorious inheritance in the saints, and his incomparably great power for us who believe. That power is like the working of his mighty strength, which he exerted in Christ when he raised him from the dead and seated him at his right hand in the heavenly realms, far above all rule and authority, power, and dominion, and every title that can be given, not only in the present age but also in the one to come. And God placed all things under his feet and appointed him to be head over everything for the church, which is his body, the fullness of him who fills everything in every way.

—Ephesians 1:15-22

In him and through faith in him we may approach God with freedom and confidence.

—Ephesians 3:12

You, dear children, are from God and have overcome them, because the one who is in you is greater than the one who is in the world.

—1 John 4:4

"I (Jesus) am coming to you now, but I say these things while I am still in the world, so that they may have the full measure of my joy within them. I have given them your word and the world has hated them, for they are not of the world any more than I am of the world. My prayer is not that you take them out of the world but that you protect them from the evil one. They are not of the world, even as I am not of it. Sanctify them by the truth; your word is truth. As you sent me into the world, I have sent them into the world. For them I sanctify myself, that they too may be truly sanctified."

—John 17:13-19

A Final Word of Encouragement from the Author

Congratulations! If you have given your life to the Lord Jesus Christ either today or some time in the past, you have made the best decision you will ever make.

If you have just made that choice, perhaps you are a little afraid right now. You might be asking yourself, "Is this real?" Scripture say there should be no doubt. If you really meant it when you asked the Lord Jesus Christ to forgive you of your sins and to come into your heart, it is a fact.

You can know with certainly that you are forgiven and, as a result of your new relationship with Christ, you can change. 1 John 1:9 tells us, "If we confess our sins, he is faithful and just and will forgive us our sins and purify us from all unrighteousness." Psalm 32:5 says, "Then I acknowledged my sin to you and did not cover up my iniquity. I said, 'I will confess my transgressions to the Lord'—and you forgave the guilt of my sin."

Even if you don't feel forgiven or see overnight change, rest assured the new beginning started the moment you asked the Lord Jesus Christ to come into your life. 2 Corinthians 5:17 says, "Therefore, if anyone (that means you) is in Christ, he is a new creation; old things have passed away; behold all things have become new."

That truth is already a reality in your life, but the new life you are living is a process. With God's help, you will need to take one small step at a time. Remember that with every tiny step you take, you are progressing toward being a new person and ultimately overcoming your anger.

Even after I gave my life to the Lord Jesus Christ in 1982, I still struggled with controlling my temper when I got mad. Just a few months after I got saved, I found myself in a challenging situation which in the past had always caused me to lose control and strike out. One of the guards at the prison thought I was trying to get smart with him. I wasn't, but the guard confronted me anyway and started hitting me in the face with his fists. When he did, my old angry attitude showed up wanting to take over. I couldn't wait for the guard to let me go so I could retaliate. As soon as he took the handcuffs off of me, I ran straight to my locker to get my homemade knife. That's when I sensed God speaking to me saying, "Eddie, stop! Don't do it." To my amazement, I didn't! Instead, I chose God's way and let the whole things drop.

You might be asking whether it was easy for me to make that choice. The answer is no. It was hard, but every time I chose to let go and let God have His way in my life, a change began to take place. It wasn't overnight, and it wasn't a major change all at once. It was only tiny steps, but each one I took helped me grow in the Lord and begin to control my anger. The same thing can happen for you. Begin today taking those tiny steps and you too will grow stronger in your relationship with the Lord Jesus Christ and in overcoming your anger.

REDEMPTION◆PRESS

To order additional copies of this book, please visit

www.redemption-press.com

Also available on Amazon.com and BarnesandNoble.com
Or by calling toll free 1-(844) 273-3336